D0995427

Money, Interest, and Policy

Money, Interest, and Policy

Dynamic General Equilibrium in a Non-Ricardian World

Jean-Pascal Bénassy

The MIT Press

Cambridge, Massachusetts

London, England

MOS 2011 00002

DUALE HOCHSCHULE
BADEN-WÜRTTEMBERG
MOSBACH
Lohrtalweg 10
74821 Mosbach

Ausgeschieden

© 2007 Massachusetts Institute of Technology

All rights reserved. No part of this book may be reproduced in any form by any electronic or mechanical means (including photocopying, recording, or information storage and retrieval) without permission in writing from the publisher.

MIT Press books may be purchased at special quantity discounts fro business or sales promotional use. For information, please email special_sales@mitpress.mit .edu or write to Special Sales Department, The MIT Press, 55 Hayward Street, Cambridge, MA 02142.

This book was set in Times New Roman on 3B2 by Asco Typesetters, Hong Kong and was printed and bound in the United States of America.

Library of Congress Cataloging-in-Publication Data

Bénassy, Jean-Pascal.
Money, interest, and policy : dynamic general equilibrium in a non-Ricardian world / Jean-Pascal Bénassy.
   p.   cm.
Includes bibliographical references and index.
ISBN-13: 978-0-262-02613-0 (alk. paper)
1. Money—Mathematical models. 2. Equilibrium (Economics)—Mathematical models. I. Title.
HG220.5.B46   2007
339.5'3—dc22   2006046859

10 9 8 7 6 5 4 3 2 1

Contents

Introduction

Monetary Economies and the Ricardian Issue

The object of this book is to construct rigorous models that bridge the current gap between a number of monetary intuitions and facts, and recent macroeconomic modeling in the area of dynamic general equilibrium. Currently the most popular models in this area are Ricardian (in a sense that will be made clear just below). Ricardian models have been successful on several points but nevertheless produce disturbing puzzles and paradoxes on a number of important monetary issues. A central theme of this book is that moving to so-called non-Ricardian models allows one to solve many of these problems in one shot.

Ricardian versus Non-Ricardian Dynamic Models

One of the most important developments in macroeconomics in recent years has been the replacement of traditional ad hoc macroeconomic models by dynamic stochastic general equilibrium (DSGE) macromodels, where all decisions are taken by fully maximizing agents (consumers and firms).

Of course there are many possible types of DSGE models as there are many types of general equilibrium models. The most popular DSGE model is a stochastic version of the famous Ramsey (1928) model. Households in the economy are represented as a homogeneous family of infinitely lived individuals. We call such economies and models Ricardian because they have the famous Ricardian equivalence property (Barro 1974), according to which, as long as the government fulfills its intertemporal budget constraint, the repartition of (lump-sum) taxes across time is irrelevant. Another striking property is that in such models bonds do not represent real wealth for households.

However, in this book by non-Ricardian we mean models where, due for example to the birth of new agents as in the overlapping generations (OLG) model of Samuelson (1958), Ricardian equivalence does not hold. In such models the precise timing of fiscal policy does matter, and government bonds, or at least a fraction of them, represent real wealth for the agents.

Ricardian Monetary Models: Puzzles and Paradoxes

When people started studying monetary phenomena within the DSGE framework, they quite naturally continued to use the Ricardian model, adding traditional devices (cash in advance, or money in the utility function) that allow money to coexist with other financial assets.

Although the Ricardian model has been successful on a number of points, it turned out that the introduction of money delivered surprising and paradoxical results on a number of important monetary issues. We mention below three examples, all of which are treated in this book:

1. The standard Ricardian model predicts that under realistic monetary processes, the nominal interest rate will go up if there is a positive shock on money. In contrast, in traditional models, and apparently in reality, the nominal interest rate goes down (the liquidity effect).
2. Following Sargent and Wallace (1975) it has been shown that in these models interest rate pegging leads to "nominal indeterminacy" (which means that if a sequence of prices is an equilibrium one, then any proportional price sequence is also an equilibrium one). This is quite bothersome since, from a normative point of view, many optimal policy packages include the "Friedman rule," according to which the nominal interest rate should be equal to zero. This means that such policies can lead to price indeterminacies.
3. Another condition for determinacy of the price level has been developed in recent years, called the fiscal theory of the price level (FTPL). FTPL says that if interest rates do not react strongly enough to inflation,

price determinacy can nevertheless be achieved if the government follows a rather adventurous fiscal policy, consisting in expanding government liabilities at such a high rate that intertemporal government solvency is achieved for a unique value of the price (hence the determinacy result). It is clearly not a policy one would want to advise.

Non-Ricardian Models: Solving the Paradoxes

These puzzles and paradoxes might cast some doubts on the relevance of the DSGE methodology for monetary economics. We take a more positive view here, and we argue that moving to non-Ricardian models can help us solve all three problems (and others) with a single modification. The modification we will implement consists in considering non-Ricardian economies by assuming (as in the real world) that new agents are born over time, whereas there are no births in the Ricardian model.

As it turns out, moving from a Ricardian to a non-Ricardian framework changes many properties:

1. In non-Ricardian models a liquidity effect naturally appears, through which an increase in the quantity of money leads to a decrease in the interest rate.
2. In non-Ricardian models price determinacy is consistent with interest rate pegging, under the condition that the pegged interest rate leads to a high enough return on financial assets.
3. In non-Ricardian models the risky policies implicitly advocated by the fiscal theory of the price level can be replaced by much more traditional policies.

The Pigou Effect

Of course, it is remarkable that the introduction of an (apparently unrelated) "demographic" assumption changes so many things in the properties of monetary models. We will see in this book that one fundamental key to the differences is the so-called Pigou effect (due to Pigou 1943) that is absent in the Ricardian model but present in the non-Ricardian one. The Pigou effect was thoroughly studied and developed by Patinkin (1956) under the name of "real balance effect," and it was central to many macroeconomic debates in the 1950s and 1960s. Unfortunately, since then it has been by and large forgotten by many theorists.

In brief, there is a Pigou effect when aggregate financial wealth matters for the behavior of agents and for the dynamics of the economy. This will be the case, for example, when the aggregate consumption depends positively on aggregate wealth. It will be shown below that the presence of this financial wealth in the dynamic equations changes many properties. The intuition here as to why a Pigou effect appears in non-Ricardian economies, whereas it is absent from the Ricardian ones, is found in Weil (1991). If one writes the intertemporal budget constraint of the government, one sees that every dollar of financial wealth is matched by an equal amount of discounted taxes. If there is a single infinitely lived family, these taxes fall 100 percent on the agents alive, so they match exactly their financial assets. As a result financial assets and taxes cancel each other, and the assets disappear from the intertemporal budget constraints and the agents' behavioral equations. Now, if there are births in this economy, the newborn agents in all future periods will pay part of these taxes, and consequently only part of the financial assets of agents currently alive will be matched by taxes. The rest will represent real wealth to them, leading to a Pigou effect.

Modeling

In this book we make a number of modeling choices. These we briefly discuss below.

The first central choice is that of the specific non-Ricardian model that we choose in order to eliminate Ricardian equivalence and obtain a Pigou effect. As indicated above, the selected model includes a "demographic" specification that allows new agents to be born over time. There are, of course, different ways to obtain a non-Ricardian economy, and one may conjecture that other such departures from a Ricardian world would lead, at least on some points, to similar results. But we will concentrate exclusively on the "demographic" aspect in order to have an homogeneous exposition.

Now there are at least two standard monetary models along this line, the overlapping generations model (in line with Samuelson 1958) and the Weil (1987, 1991) model. As we will see below, the Weil model has the great advantage of "nesting" the traditional Ricardian model when the birth rate is taken equal to zero, so the role of the non-Ricardian assumption appears crystal clear. We use this model in chapters 2 through 6. However, because in this model an infinity of generations coexist at the same time in the economy, the computations can become too complex, so in chapters 7 through 10, where optimal policy in economies hit by stochastic shocks is studied, we move to a simpler OLG model.

Finally, although the original Weil model is in continuous time, we use instead a discrete time version. There are two reasons for that. The first is that our models are meant to be compared with models in the DSGE tradition, and these models are almost exclusively set in discrete time. The second is that since the OLG model in part III is by nature in discrete time, it was preferable for the homogeneity of exposition to set the Weil model in discrete time as well.

Plan of the Book

This book has been divided into three homogeneous parts. Part I lays the groundwork by comparing and opposing polar Ricardian and non-Ricardian models, and introducing elements of synthesis.

Chapter 1 studies in parallel a Ricardian model with an infinitely lived representative agent and an overlapping generations model. It shows that these two models deliver dramatically different answers with respect to central issues in monetary theory like price determinacy or liquidity effects. These differences are attributed to the presence (or absence) of a Pigou effect.

Chapter 2 presents the Weil (1987, 1991) model that is used in chapters 3 through 6, and that is somehow a synthesis of the two previous models. It is a model that includes both infinite lives and birth of new agents. It has the advantage of "nesting" the Ricardian model while displaying the Pigou effect for positive rates of birth. Chapter 2 studies more closely how the Pigou effect arises in agents' behavioral equations (e.g., in the aggregate consumption function) and in the dynamic equations.

Part II considers a number of "positive" issues in monetary theory, using the unified non-Ricardian framework of the Weil model. The topics studied are notably (1) liquidity effects, (2) interest rate rules, the Taylor principle and price determinacy, (3) global determinacy, and (4) the fiscal theory of the price level.

Chapter 3 introduces a new mechanism by which liquidity effects, namely the negative response of the nominal interest rate to monetary injections, can be integrated into dynamic stochastic general equilibrium (DSGE) models. As it turns out, this liquidity effect has been found diffcult to obtain in standard monetary DSGE models because of an "inflationary expectations effect," which can raise the nominal interest rate in response to a monetary injection. In chapter 3 we explore a new non-Ricardian argument. For that we use a stochastic version of the Weil model. We then compute an explicit expression for the interest rate. It consists of two terms. The first is the inflationary expectations term. The second term corresponds to the traditional liquidity effect and leads to a decrease in the interest rate. The relative weight between the two terms is a synthetic parameter that depends, inter alia, on the rate of growth of the population. For a high enough value of the parameter, the liquidity effect dominates and is persistent.

Chapter 4 studies under which conditions interest rate rules à la Taylor (1993) can lead to local price determinacy, and shows that these conditions change dramatically when one moves from a Ricardian to a non-Ricardian framework. The chapter notably studies the famous Taylor principle, which says that if the nominal interest rate responds to inflation, price determinacy will be ensured if the elasticity of response to inflation is more than hundred percent. We first check that this principle holds indeed in the Ricardian version of the model. We then move to a non-Ricardian framework, and show that the determinacy conditions change totally. The main condition is akin to Wallace's (1980) condition for the viability of money in an OLG framework, and says that the real interest earned on financial assets should be superior to the real interest rate prevailing in the model without births. We call this the financial dominance criterion, which is quite different from the traditional determinacy conditions.

Chapter 5 investigates the issue of global determinacy. The preceding chapter showed the importance of the financial dominance criterion in ensuring local determinacy when monetary policy is defined by a "Taylor rule," whereby the nominal interest rate responds to the inflation rate. But it is well known that local determinacy does not imply global determinacy, and that the conditions for the two can be quite different. So we investigate the issue of global determinacy and find that the financial dominance criterion is essential for global determinacy. That is, if financial dominance is satisfied for all values of the inflation rate, global determinacy is ensured.

Chapter 6 examines a most intriguing theory of fiscal policy and price determinacy, which has developed lately under the name of fiscal theory of the price level (FTPL). This theory says that if the monetary policy does not satisfy the Taylor principle (e.g., if the interest rate is pegged), then an "adequate" fiscal policy can nevertheless reestablish price determinacy. The problem is that this "adequate" fiscal policy is a risky one, as it consists in expanding public debt in such a way that government does not satisfy its long-term budget constraint, except for one single value of the initial price (hence the determinacy result). We see in this chapter that this result is actually specific to the Ricardian version of the model. When one moves to a non-Ricardian framework, the policy prescriptions are much more reasonable, and in particular consistent with a nonexplosive debt policy by government. Price determinacy can occur, for example, when the expansion of fiscal liabilities is lower than a certain level, and not higher, as in the FTPL.

Part III of the book is devoted to the analysis of optimal monetary and fiscal policies, with a special emphasis on optimal interest rate rules. As we indicate above, we use in this part a simple overlapping generations model in the spirit of Samuelson (1958).

Chapter 7 describes the model used in chapters 7 through 10. It is an OLG model with money and production. Chapter 7 builds the model, derives the Walrasian equilibrium, and describes the optimality criterion used in these four chapters. A first application is made in deriving the optimal monetary and fiscal policies in a Walrasian framework. The optimal policies turn out to satisfy the two "Friedman rules" (Friedman 1969): the nominal interest rate is set at zero, while some nominal aggregate grows (actually decreases) at rate β, where β is the discount rate in the optimality criterion.

Chapter 8 studies the much debated issue of the optimality of policy activism, namely whether government policies should respond to economic events, and, if yes, how? Until the early 1970s views on this matter were dominated by Keynesian thinking, according to which wage (or price) rigidities provide a strong case for activist countercyclical demand policies. But an important critique was put forward by Sargent and Wallace (1975). They argue that in most traditional Keynesian models policy effectiveness is essentially due to an "informational advantage" implicitly conferred to the government in these models. More precisely, the government is allowed to react to some "recent" shocks while the private sector is locked into "old" wage or price contracts. Now, if the government is not allowed to use more information about shocks than the private sector, then government policies become "ineffective." This question of ineffectiveness is then re-examined in a rigorous "structural" maximizing model with preset wages or prices. In this case the government is "less informed" than the private sector, in the sense that the government takes its policy actions on the basis of information that is never superior to that of the private sector. Despite these restrictions we find that the optimal policy is an activist one. For example, the optimal fiscal policy is counter-cyclical, in the sense that the fiscal transfers are negatively related to past demand shocks.

Chapter 9 bridges the gap between the optimal policy results of chapter 8 and the literature on optimal interest rate rules. Indeed in the model of chapter 8, although it is optimal to have an activist policy, the monetary part of this policy is actually "passive," since the nominal interest rate remains pegged at zero (the Friedman rule). Many recent writers have insisted instead on the necessity of an "active" interest rate policy. The two views can actually be reconciled if one realizes that the delays for implementing fiscal policy are actually much longer than those for interest rate policy. So in this chapter we take this idea to the extreme and investigate what is the optimal interest rate rule when fiscal policy is too slow to be used. We find that the optimal interest rate rule becomes activist and reacts to the same shocks as fiscal policy did in chapter 8.

Chapter 10 investigates optimal interest rate rules when these take the form of "Taylor rules," which are functions of the inflation rate. The chapter particularly scrutinizes the issue of the Taylor principle, according to which the nominal interest rate should respond more than one for one to inflation. We develop a simple model for which explicit solutions of the optimal interest rate rules can be computed. We particularly study how the optimal degree of response to inflation depends on (1) the autocorrelation of shocks, (2) the degree of rigidity of prices (in a model with staggered prices), and (3) the particular measure of inflation that is used (current versus expected). We find that the corresponding elasticity can be smaller or greater than one, depending on the values of the relevant parameters, and thus not systematically greater than one, as the Taylor principle suggests.

A Reading Guide

This book is a short one. It is of course best to read it sequentially. For the impatient reader, however, we have a few hints.

Parts II and III can be read independently. Within each of these parts sequential reading is strongly advised, although chapters 3 and 10 can, for the most part, be read independently.

A number of results of the various models are presented in the form of propositions. This system is meant to facilitate quick reading, since the proofs of these propositions can be skipped in a first reading without loss of continuity.

In order not to burden the text, references in the main text have been kept to a strict minimum. Relevant references are gathered at the end of each chapter.

Acknowledgments

I owe a great debt to Michel Guillard and Philippe Weil, whose comments on an earlier version of this book led to many improvements. Any remaining deficiencies are of course mine.

Part I

Ricardian and Non-Ricardian
Economies

1

The Ricardian Issue and the Pigou Effect

1.1 Introduction

Since the aim of this book is to highlight the distinction between Ricardian and non-Ricardian models, we start in this chapter by pointing out the differences using two polar models: first we describe a standard Ricardian monetary model, and next a non-Ricardian monetary model based on an overlapping generations structure. As will become apparent, the differences are large between the two types of models.

We will further see that these differences are particularly connected to the presence or absence of a Pigou effect (Pigou 1943; Patinkin 1956). We will see why this Pigou effect, which is present in the overlapping generations model, disappears completely from the Ricardian one.

1.2 The Traditional Ricardian Model

The standard monetary Ricardian model is mainly associated with the work of Ramsey (1928), Sidrauski (1967), and Brock (1974, 1975). In this model the consumer side is represented by a single dynasty of identical infinitely lived households. There are no births, and no one ever dies.

1.2.1   Households

In each period t the representative household receives an exogenous real income Y_t and consumes an amount C_t. It chooses the sequence of its consumptions so as to maximize an intertemporal utility function. In a particular period t, the utility of the representative household from period t onward is

$$U_t = \sum_{s=t}^{\infty} \beta^{s-t} \log C_s \tag{1}$$

This household is submitted in each period to a cash in advance constraint, à la Clower (1967),

$$P_t C_t \leq M_t \qquad \forall t \tag{2}$$

The household enters period t with a financial wealth Ω_t. Things happen in two successive steps. The household first visits the bonds market where it splits this wealth between bonds B_t (which it lends at the nominal interest rate i_t) and money M_t:

$$M_t + B_t = \Omega_t \tag{3}$$

Next, the goods market opens, and the household sells its endowment Y_t, pays taxes T_t in real terms and consumes C_t, subject to the cash constraint (2). Consequently its financial wealth at the beginning of the next period Ω_{t+1} is given by the budget constraint

$$\Omega_{t+1} = (1 + i_t)B_t + M_t + P_t Y_t - P_t T_t - P_t C_t \tag{4}$$

which, using (3), can be rewritten as

$$\Omega_{t+1} = (1 + i_t)\Omega_t - i_t M_t + P_t Y_t - P_t T_t - P_t C_t \tag{5}$$

1.2.2   Government

Another important part of the model is the government. The households' financial wealth Ω_t has as a counterpart an identical amount Ω_t of financial liabilities of the government. The evolution of these liabilities is described by the government's budget constraint[1]

$$\Omega_{t+1} = (1 + i_t)\Omega_t - i_t M_t - P_t T_t \tag{6}$$

The government has two types of policy instruments: fiscal policy, which consists in setting taxes T_t (expressed in real terms) and monetary policy. Monetary policy can take several forms. Two classic monetary policies are as follows:

1. Setting the interest rate i_t, and letting the market determine M_t.
2. Setting the quantity of money M_t, and letting the market equilibrium determine i_t.

We will consider both policies in what follows. All policies, fiscal and monetary, are announced at the beginning of each period.

1.2.3 First-Order Conditions

We first derive the first-order conditions. Assume that i_t is strictly positive. Then the household will always want to satisfy exactly the cash in advance constraint (2) so that $M_t = P_t C_t$. The budget constraint (5) then becomes

$$\Omega_{t+1} = (1 + i_t)\Omega_t + P_t Y_t - P_t T_t - (1 + i_t)P_t C_t \tag{7}$$

Maximizing the utility function (1) subject to the sequence of budget constraints (7) yields the following first-order condition:

$$\frac{1}{P_t C_t} = \beta(1 + i_t)E_t\left(\frac{1}{P_{t+1}C_{t+1}}\right) \tag{8}$$

1.3 Monetary Puzzles

We now consider two standard monetary experiments, and see that the Ricardian model delivers surprising answers. We will see in section

---

1. We omit here government spending, since at this point it would only complicate notation. Appendix A at the end of this chapter shows how formulas change when government spending is included.

1.4 that an overlapping generations model with similar features instead delivers the answers one would expect.

1.3.1   Interest Rate Pegging and Nominal Price Indeterminacy

There is nominal indeterminacy if, whenever a price sequence is an equilibrium, then any price sequence multiple of the first one is also an equilibrium. It was first pointed out by Sargent and Wallace (1975) that pegging nominal interest rates could lead to such nominal indeterminacy. At the time they did not use a model with explicit intertemporal maximization, so it is useful to restate the problem in the framework of the maximizing model just described. To make things simpler, assume that there is no uncertainty and that the nominal interest rate is pegged at the value i_t in period t. The first-order condition (8) is then rewritten as

$$\frac{1}{P_t C_t} = \beta(1 + i_t)\frac{1}{P_{t+1} C_{t+1}} \tag{9}$$

It is shown below that these first order conditions together with the intertemporal budget constraint of the consumer yield the following consumption function (equation 45):

$$D_t P_t C_t = (1 - \beta)\sum_{s=t}^{\infty} D_s P_s Y_s \tag{10}$$

where the D_t's are discount rates equal to

$$D_t = \prod_{s=0}^{t-1}\frac{1}{1 + i_s} \quad D_0 = 1 \tag{11}$$

Since markets clear, $C_t = Y_t$ for all t. Then, inserting this into (10), we obtain the equilibrium equations

$$D_t P_t Y_t = (1 - \beta)\sum_{s=t}^{\infty} D_s P_s Y_s \quad \forall t \tag{12}$$

We see first that financial wealth Ω_t does not appear in these equations, so that there is no Pigou effect. Also equations (12) are homogeneous of degree 1 in prices, so that if a sequence P_t is a solution of all these equations, then any sequence multiple of that one will also be a solution. There is thus nominal indeterminacy, and the Sargent and Wallace (1975) result is valid in this maximizing framework.

We can now compute relative intertemporal prices. Replacing C_t and C_{t+1} by Y_t and Y_{t+1} in equation (9) we find that

$$\frac{P_{t+1}}{P_t} = \beta(1 + i_t)\frac{Y_t}{Y_{t+1}} \tag{13}$$

We then see that although absolute prices are indeterminate, setting nominal interest rates determines the ratios between intertemporal prices P_{t+1}/P_t. We can also compute the net and gross real interest rate r_t and R_t:

$$1 + r_t = R_t = \frac{(1 + i_t)P_t}{P_{t+1}} = \frac{1}{\beta}\frac{Y_{t+1}}{Y_t} \tag{14}$$

If we assume, as we will do in subsequent chapters, that output per head grows at the rate ζ, then $Y_{t+1}/Y_t = \zeta$ and

$$1 + r_t = R_t = \frac{\zeta}{\beta} \tag{15}$$

1.3.2   The Liquidity Puzzle

Let us now consider another traditional monetary experiment. This time the quantity of money, not the interest rate, is the operating monetary variable. We assume that the quantity of money follows a stochastic process, and we would like to know what is the response of the nominal interest rate to a monetary expansion.

The traditional answer to this question is that there is a "liquidity effect," meaning a negative response of the nominal interest rate to monetary injections. That liquidity effect was already present in the famous IS-LM model, and it appears to be found in the data (e.g., see Christiano, Eichenbaum, and Evans 1997). As it turns out, the liquidity effect is difficult to obtain in standard monetary DSGE models. This is because of an inflationary expectations effect that actually raises the nominal interest rate in response to a monetary injection.

We now briefly outline the mechanism behind this inflationary expectations effect. It is found in the data that money increases are positively correlated in time. As an unexpected money increase occurs, this creates the expectation of further money increases in the future, which will itself create the expectation of future inflation. By Fisher's equation, the nominal interest rate is the sum of expected inflation and the real interest rate, and ceteris paribus, this will raise the nominal interest rate.

To make things more formal, consider the first-order condition (8). Assume that interest rates are positive. So the cash-in-advance constraint (2) is satisfied with equality in all periods, and the first-order condition is rewritten as

$$\frac{1}{M_t} = \beta(1 + i_t)E_t\left(\frac{1}{M_{t+1}}\right) \tag{16}$$

This equation can be immediately solved for the interest rate as

$$\frac{1}{1 + i_t} = \beta E_t\left(\frac{M_t}{M_{t+1}}\right) \tag{17}$$

In order to find the effect of a monetary shock, we need to know the response of $E_t(M_t/M_{t+1})$ to a shock on M_t. Many authors describe the monetary process under the form of an autoregressive process:

$$\log\left(\frac{M_t}{M_{t-1}}\right) = \frac{\varepsilon_t}{1 - \rho\mathcal{L}}, \qquad 0 \leq \rho < 1 \tag{18}$$

In the formula above, ε_t is an i.i.d. stochastic variable and $\mathcal{L}$ is the lag operator which, for any time series x_t, is defined by

$$\mathcal{L}^j x_t = x_{t-j} \tag{19}$$

Most empirical evaluations find a value of ρ around 0.5. In such a case $E_t(M_t/M_{t+1})$ is decreasing in M_t and therefore the nominal interest rate will *increase* in response to a positive monetary shock. This is the inflationary expectations effect, which causes the nominal interest rate to be pushed in a direction opposite to that predicted by the traditional liquidity effect.

1.4 An Overlapping Generations Model

We will now consider an alternative model, a monetary overlapping generations model in the tradition of Samuelson (1958). We will see that it delivers answers strikingly different from those obtained in the Ricardian model.

1.4.1 The Model

The household side is represented by overlapping generations of consumers. Households born in period t live for two periods, t and $t+1$, and receive real income Y_t when young. They consume C_{1t} in period t, C_{2t+1} in period $t+1$, and their utility is

$$U_t = \alpha \log C_{1t} + \log C_{2t+1} \tag{20}$$

In each period of its life a household born in period t is submitted to a cash-in-advance constraint

$$P_t C_{1t} \leq M_{1t}, \quad P_{t+1} C_{2t+1} \leq M_{2t+1} \tag{21}$$

Total consumption and money are

$$C_t = C_{1t} + C_{2t}, \quad M_t = M_{1t} + M_{2t} \tag{22}$$

As in the previous Ricardian model, let us call Ω_t the total amount of financial assets that the agents have at the beginning of period t. Since young households are born without any assets, Ω_t is entirely in the hands of old households. To simplify the exposition, we assume that taxes T_t are levied only on young households.

1.4.2 Equilibrium

Let us start with the old households who arrive in period t with financial assets Ω_t. In view of the 100 percent cash-in-advance constraint (formula 21), their consumption is equal to

$$C_{2t} = \frac{\Omega_t}{P_t} \tag{23}$$

Let us now study the problem of the young household. If it consumes C_{1t} in the first period, it must acquire a quantity of money $P_t C_{1t}$ to satisfy its cash-in-advance constraint, and therefore borrow $P_t C_{1t}$ from the central bank so that it holds a quantity of money and bonds:

$$M_{1t} = P_t C_{1t} \quad \text{and} \quad B_{1t} = -P_t C_{1t} \tag{24}$$

At the end of period t it will hold (and transfer to period $t + 1$) a quantity of financial assets equal to

$$\Omega_{t+1} = M_{1t} + (1 + i_t)B_{1t} + P_t Y_t - P_t T_t - P_t C_{1t}$$

$$= P_t Y_t - P_t T_t - (1 + i_t)P_t C_{1t} \tag{25}$$

Second-period consumption is obtained by combining (23) and (25) as

$$C_{2t+1} = \frac{\Omega_{t+1}}{P_{t+1}} = \frac{P_t Y_t - P_t T_t - (1 + i_t)P_t C_{1t}}{P_{t+1}} \tag{26}$$

Inserting (26) into the utility function (20), we find that the young household will choose its first period consumption C_{1t} so as to maximize

$$\alpha \log C_{1t} + \log[P_t Y_t - P_t T_t - (1 + i_t)P_t C_{1t}] \tag{27}$$

The first-order condition for C_{1t} is

$$\frac{\alpha}{C_{1t}} = \frac{(1 + i_t)P_t}{P_t Y_t - P_t T_t - (1 + i_t)P_t C_{1t}} \tag{28}$$

which yields the first-period consumption function

$$C_{1t} = \frac{\alpha}{1 + \alpha} \frac{Y_t - T_t}{1 + i_t} \tag{29}$$

Combining (29) with (23), we write total consumption as

$$C_t = C_{1t} + C_{2t} = \frac{\alpha}{1 + \alpha} \frac{Y_t - T_t}{1 + i_t} + \frac{\Omega_t}{P_t} \tag{30}$$

The equation of equilibrium on the goods market is $C_t = Y_t$, which yields

$$Y_t = \frac{\alpha}{1+\alpha} \frac{Y_t - T_t}{1+i_t} + \frac{\Omega_t}{P_t} \tag{31}$$

We have also a second equilibrium equation, which says that, in view of the cash-in-advance constraint (21), the total quantity of money M_t is equal to $P_t C_t$, that is,

$$M_t = P_t Y_t \tag{32}$$

Note that the two equations (31) and (32) somehow correspond to traditional *IS* and *LM* equations.

1.4.3 Interest Pegging and Price Determinacy

Let us consider again the issue of price determinacy under interest rate pegging, and assume that the nominal interest rate is exogenously given at the level i_t in period t. We can solve equation (31) for the price level:

$$P_t = \frac{(1+\alpha)(1+i_t)\Omega_t}{(1+i_t+\alpha i_t)Y_t + \alpha T_t} \tag{33}$$

We see that the price level is fully determinate. We further see that

$$\frac{\partial P_t}{\partial i_t} = \frac{-\alpha(1+\alpha)\Omega_t(Y_t - T_t)}{[(1+i_t+\alpha i_t)Y_t + \alpha T_t]^2} < 0 \tag{34}$$

so that the price depends negatively on the interest rate, as is usually expected.

1.4.4 The Liquidity Effect

Let us now assume that the quantity of money is exogenous. We combine equations (31) and (32) and solve for the interest rate. We find[2] that

---

2. Note that $M_t - \Omega_t$ in the denominator of the last fraction is always positive since it is equal to $P_t C_{1t}$.

$$1 + i_t = \frac{\alpha}{1 + \alpha} \frac{Y_t - T_t}{Y_t} \frac{M_t}{M_t - \Omega_t} \qquad (35)$$

There is clearly a liquidity effect, since

$$\frac{\partial i_t}{\partial M_t} = -\frac{\alpha}{1 + \alpha} \frac{Y_t - T_t}{Y_t} \frac{\Omega_t}{\left(M_t - \Omega_t\right)^2} < 0 \qquad (36)$$

1.4.5   A Summary

We have just seen that the two models we presented display strikingly different properties:

1. In the case of a nominal interest rate peg, the Ricardian model displays nominal indeterminacy, whereas in the OLG model the price level is fully determinate.
2. In the Ricardian model, a positive shock on money leads to a nominal interest rate increase but to a decrease in the OLG model.

We will argue below that these important differences are related to the presence of a Pigou effect in the OLG model and its absence in the Ricardian model.

1.5   The Pigou Effect

Let us say that a Pigou effect is present if the amount of financial assets Ω_t is considered, at least partly, as wealth by the households. In particular, Ω_t will have a positive influence on consumption. We know from equation (30) that there is such a Pigou effect in the overlapping generations model. We know also from equations (33) and (36) that both the price determinacy and the liquidity effect in the OLG model are due to the presence of Ω_t in the central equilibrium equation (31).

However, in the Ricardian model, we saw that although Ω_t appears in budget constraints such as (5), it disappears in the consumption function (equation 10) or in the equilibrium equations (equation 12), and this leads to the bizarre properties of the Ricardian model. We will now find out why this happens.

1.5.1 The Intertemporal Budget Constraint

We want to investigate why in the Ricardian model nominal assets appear in the period by period budget constraints but do not seem to have any role in the end. Let us first recall the budget constraint for period t:

$$\Omega_{t+1} = (1 + i_t)\Omega_t + P_t Y_t - P_t T_t - (1 + i_t)P_t C_t \qquad (37)$$

Note that Ω_t still appears at this stage. Next, to show why it disappears in the end, we derive the intertemporal budget constraint of the household. Recall that the discount factors are

$$D_t = \prod_{s=0}^{t-1} \frac{1}{1 + i_s}, \quad D_0 = 1 \qquad (38)$$

Consider the household's budget equation (37) for period s. Multiplying it by D_{s+1} it becomes:

$$D_{s+1}\Omega_{s+1} = D_s\Omega_s + D_{s+1}P_s Y_s - D_{s+1}P_s T_s - D_s P_s C_s \qquad (39)$$

If we sum all discounted budget constraints (39) from time t to infinity, and assume that $D_s\Omega_s$ goes to zero as s goes to infinity (a usual transversality condition), we have the intertemporal budget constraint of the household as

$$\sum_{s=t}^{\infty} D_s P_s C_s = D_t\Omega_t + \sum_{s=t}^{\infty} D_{s+1}P_s Y_s - \sum_{s=t}^{\infty} D_{s+1}P_s T_s \qquad (40)$$

In (40) aggregate financial wealth Ω_t is still present on the right hand side. This might lead us to believe that nominal assets can play a role, but such reasoning is misleading because it treats initial financial wealth Ω_t and the sequence of taxes T_s, $s \geq t$ as independent. They are instead closely linked through the government's intertemporal budget constraint. To see how, we have to evaluate the discounted value of taxes. First, we consider the government's budget constraint (equation 6) for period s:

$$\Omega_{s+1} = (1 + i_s)\Omega_s - i_s M_s - P_s T_s \qquad (41)$$

Next, we multiply (41) by D_{s+1}, and use $M_s = P_s C_s = P_s Y_s$:

$$D_{s+1}\Omega_{s+1} = D_s\Omega_s - (D_s - D_{s+1})P_s Y_s - D_{s+1}P_s T_s \qquad (42)$$

Then, we sum all these equalities from time t to infinity:

$$\sum_{s=t}^{\infty} D_{s+1} P_s T_s = D_t \Omega_t - \sum_{s=t}^{\infty}(D_s - D_{s+1})P_s Y_s \qquad (43)$$

Notice that any increase in the value of nominal assets Ω_t is matched by an identical increase in the discounted value of taxes. If we insert this value of discounted taxes (43) into the household's intertemporal budget constraint (40), we find that

$$\sum_{s=t}^{\infty} D_s P_s C_s = \sum_{s=t}^{\infty} D_s P_s Y_s \qquad (44)$$

We see that the financial assets have completely disappeared from the intertemporal budget constraint! Now let us maximize the utility function (1) subject to this budget constraint. We obtain the consumption function:

$$D_t P_t C_t = (1 - \beta) \sum_{s=t}^{\infty} D_s P_s Y_s \qquad (45)$$

We see that Ω_t appears neither in the budget constraint (44) nor in the consumption function (45). There is no Pigou effect in the Ricardian model, contrary to what happens in the OLG model.

So what we have found is that the Ricardian intuition, which was usually applied to show that real bonds are not real wealth (Barro 1974), can be applied to financial assets as well (Weil 1991).

1.5.2   The Individual Value of Money

We have just seen that aggregate financial assets are somehow not counted in the wealth of society. A question we will further pursue, although it does not play a role in what follows, is: Do individual financial assets represent wealth for the individual households who hold them? To explore this question, we need to modify a little our framework. We now assume there are N households in the economy. These households all have the same utility function (1); they receive each the same income y_t and transfers τ_t, which are simply aggregate income and transfers divided by N:

$$y_t = \frac{Y_t}{N}, \quad \tau_t = \frac{T_t}{N} \tag{46}$$

However, assume that, because of different histories, each household i, $i \in [1, N]$, has a different amount of financial assets, denoted as ω_{it}. Let us denote by c_{it} the consumption of agent i in period t. By the same method as the one that led to equation (40), we find that the intertemporal budget constraint of agent i is

$$\sum_{s=t}^{\infty} D_s P_s c_{is} = D_t \omega_{it} + \sum_{s=t}^{\infty} D_{s+1} P_s y_s - \sum_{s=t}^{\infty} D_{s+1} P_s \tau_s \tag{47}$$

Next we divide the government's intertemporal budget constraint by N:

$$\sum_{s=t}^{\infty} D_{s+1} P_s \tau_s = \frac{D_t \Omega_t}{N} - \sum_{s=t}^{\infty} (D_s - D_{s+1}) P_s y_s \tag{48}$$

We combine these two relations to obtain

$$\sum_{s=t}^{\infty} D_s P_s c_{is} = D_t \omega_{it} - \frac{D_t \Omega_t}{N} + \sum_{s=t}^{\infty} D_s P_s y_s \tag{49}$$

We find that individual holdings of financial assets ω_{it} do have private value to those holding the assets, but they have also a *negative* value for other agents via the second term of the right-hand side. The representative individual case we had considered before corresponds to $\omega_{it} = \Omega_t/N$, so the two first terms cancel each other.

1.6   Conclusions

We studied in this chapter two polar monetary models, a Ricardian one (the Ramsey-Sidrauski-Brock model) and a non-Ricardian one (the overlapping generations model), and we found some striking differences.

On the issue of price determinacy under interest rate pegging, we found that there is nominal indeterminacy in the Ricardian model and full determinacy in the OLG model. On the effect of a monetary expansion on the nominal interest rate, we found that this led to an increase of the nominal interest rate in the Ricardian model but a decrease in the OLG model. As we will see in later chapters, there are still more important differences of this type.

We also saw that a major difference between the two models was the presence of a Pigou effect in the OLG model and its absence in the Ricardian model. However, a problem with this comparison is a discontinuity between the two models, in that there is no formulation that includes both cases. That is why in the next chapter we will describe a model due to Weil (1987, 1991) that is a non-Ricardian model with properties similar to the OLG model but that includes the Ricardian model above as a particular case.

1.7   References

The Pigou effect is due to Pigou (1943). The significance of this effect was notably emphasized by Patinkin (1956) under the name of "real balance effect." The Pigou effect has been analyzed in intertemporal maximizing models by Weil (1987, 1991).

The Ricardian model with the infinitely lived consumer is due notably to the work of Ramsey (1928), Sidrauski (1967), and Brock (1974, 1975). The overlapping generations model was developed by Allais (1947), Samuelson (1958), and Diamond (1965).

The difference between Ricardian and non-Ricardian models, notably for fiscal policy was studied by Barro (1974), who notably asked whether real bonds are net wealth.

The cash-in-advance constraint is due to Clower (1967). In the original version the consumer had to carry cash from the previous period in order to consume. The timing we use (Helpman, 1981, Lucas, 1982), allows newborn agents to have positive consumption, a useful feature since the models we employ in this book will have newborn agents.

The price indeterminacy issue was uncovered by Sargent and Wallace (1975). A useful taxonomy of the various cases of indeterminacy is found in McCallum (1986).

The liquidity effect dates back to Keynes (1936) and Hicks (1937). A recent appraisal is found in Christiano, Eichenbaum, and Evans (1997).

Appendix A: Government Spending

Some of the equations presented in this chapter can be modified to the case where the government spends an amount G_t in real terms.

The Ricardian Model

The first modification concerns the government budget constraint (equation 6), which is now

$$\Omega_{t+1} = (1 + i_t)\Omega_t - i_t M_t - P_t T_t + P_t G_t \tag{50}$$

The condition of equilibrium on the goods market, which was $Y_t = C_t$, becomes

$$Y_t = C_t + G_t \tag{51}$$

The other basic formulas remain the same. Formula (13) relating prices intertemporally becomes

$$\frac{P_{t+1}}{P_t} = \beta(1 + i_t)\frac{Y_t - G_t}{Y_{t+1} - G_{t+1}} \tag{52}$$

and formula (17) giving the interest rate does not change:

$$\frac{1}{1 + i_t} = \beta E_t\left(\frac{M_t}{M_{t+1}}\right) \tag{53}$$

The OLG Model

The consumption functions giving C_{1t} and C_{2t} are the same, but there is a new goods market equilibrium equation:

$$C_t + G_t = C_{1t} + C_{2t} + G_t = Y_t \tag{54}$$

So equation (31) becomes

$$Y_t = \frac{\alpha}{1+\alpha} \frac{Y_t - T_t}{1 + i_t} + \frac{\Omega_t}{P_t} + G_t \tag{55}$$

We can add a second equilibrium equation saying that the total quantity of money M_t is equal to $P_t C_t$, that is, in view of (51):

$$M_t = P_t C_t = P_t(Y_t - G_t) \tag{56}$$

Then from (55) we can deduce the equation for the price level as

$$P_t = \frac{(1+\alpha)(1+i_t)\Omega_t}{(1+\alpha)(1+i_t)(Y_t - G_t) - \alpha(Y_t - T_t)} \tag{57}$$

Clearly, the price level is determinate, and further

$$\frac{\partial P_t}{\partial i_t} = \frac{-\alpha(1+\alpha)\Omega_t(Y_t - T_t)}{[(1+\alpha)(1+i_t)(Y_t - G_t) - \alpha(Y_t - T_t)]^2} < 0 \tag{58}$$

So the price depends negatively on the interest rate, as in the case without government spending. Finally, combining (55) and (56), we obtain the equation giving the interest rate:

$$1 + i_t = \frac{\alpha}{1+\alpha} \frac{Y_t - T_t}{Y_t - G_t} \frac{M_t}{M_t - \Omega_t} \tag{59}$$

There is again clearly a liquidity effect, since

$$\frac{\partial i_t}{\partial M_t} = -\frac{\alpha}{1+\alpha} \frac{Y_t - T_t}{Y_t - G_t} \frac{\Omega_t}{(M_t - \Omega_t)^2} < 0 \tag{60}$$

Appendix B: Money in the Utility Function

We will treat here the Ricardian model with a family of representative infinitely lived agents and with money in the utility function, in the tradition of Sidrauski (1967) and Brock (1974, 1975).

The Model

Assume the following simple utility:

$$U_t = \sum_{s=t}^{\infty} \beta^{s-t} \left[\vartheta \log C_s + (1 - \vartheta) \log \frac{M_s}{P_s} \right] \tag{61}$$

In period t households are endowed with a quantity Y_t of the single consumption good. The household consumes C_t of it and government purchases a quantity G_t. The condition of equilibrium on the goods market is

$$C_t + G_t = Y_t \tag{62}$$

The household enters period t with an accumulated financial wealth Ω_t. It sells its endowment Y_t, pays taxes T_t in real terms, and consumes C_t. What is left is allocated between money M_t and bonds B_t according to the following budget constraint:

$$M_t + B_t = \Omega_t + P_t Y_t - P_t T_t - P_t C_t \tag{63}$$

Financial wealth in the next period is given by

$$\Omega_{t+1} = (1 + i_t) B_t + M_t \tag{64}$$

Combining these two relations, we obtain the equation giving the evolution of financial wealth between two successive periods:

$$\Omega_{t+1} = (1 + i_t) \left(\Omega_t + P_t Y_t - P_t T_t - P_t C_t - \frac{i_t}{1 + i_t} M_t \right) \tag{65}$$

On the government side, the sum of money and bonds is equal to the sum of Ω_t and government's deficit in period t

$$M_t + B_t = \Omega_t + P_t G_t - P_t T_t \tag{66}$$

The government's liabilities Ω_t evolve according to the government's dynamic budget constraint:

$$\Omega_{t+1} = (1 + i_t) \left(\Omega_t + P_t G_t - P_t T_t - \frac{i_t}{1 + i_t} M_t \right) \tag{67}$$

Dynamics

First, we apply the interest factor D_{s+1} to the household's budget constraint (65) for period s:

$$D_{s+1}\Omega_{s+1} = D_s\Omega_s + D_sP_sY_s - D_sP_sT_s - D_sP_sC_s - D_s\frac{i_s}{1+i_s}M_s \qquad (68)$$

If we sum all budget constraints (68) from time t to infinity, and assume that $D_s\Omega_s$ goes to zero as s goes to infinity, we obtain the intertemporal budget constraint of the household:

$$\sum_{s=t}^{\infty} D_sP_sC_s + \sum_{s=t}^{\infty} D_s\frac{i_s}{1+i_s}M_s = D_t\Omega_t + \sum_{s=t}^{\infty} D_sP_s(Y_s - T_s) \qquad (69)$$

Then, maximizing the utility function (61) subject to this budget constraint, we obtain, in particular, the consumption and money demands for period t:

$$D_tP_tC_t = \vartheta(1-\beta)\left[D_t\Omega_t + \sum_{s=t}^{\infty} D_sP_s(Y_s - T_s)\right] \qquad (70)$$

$$D_t\frac{i_t}{1+i_t}M_t = (1-\vartheta)(1-\beta)\left[D_t\Omega_t + \sum_{s=t}^{\infty} D_sP_s(Y_s - T_s)\right] \qquad (71)$$

Second, we consider the government's budget constraint (67) for period s, and multiply it by the discount factor D_{s+1}:

$$D_{s+1}\Omega_{s+1} = D_s\Omega_s + D_sP_sG_s - D_sP_sT_s - D_s\frac{i_s}{1+i_s}M_s \qquad (72)$$

Summing all these budget constraints, and assuming that $D_s\Omega_s$ goes to zero as time goes to infinity, we obtain the intertemporal budget constraint of the government:

$$\sum_{s=t}^{\infty} D_sP_sT_s + \sum_{s=t}^{\infty} D_s\frac{i_s}{1+i_s}M_s = D_t\Omega_t + \sum_{s=t}^{\infty} D_sP_sG_s \qquad (73)$$

We see that discounted tax liabilities increase one for one with initial wealth Ω_t. As a consequence Ω_t will completely disappear. Indeed, if we insert the value of taxes given by (73) into (70) and (71), we obtain

$$D_t P_t C_t = \vartheta(1-\beta)\left[\sum_{s=t}^{\infty} D_s P_s (Y_s - G_s) + \sum_{s=t}^{\infty} D_s \frac{i_s}{1+i_s} M_s\right] \qquad (74)$$

$$D_t \frac{i_t}{1+i_t} M_t = \frac{1-\vartheta}{\vartheta} D_t P_t C_t \qquad (75)$$

The full equilibrium is obtained by inserting into (74) and (75) the equilibrium conditions $C_t = Y_t - G_t$ at each date. This yields

$$D_t P_t (Y_t - G_t) = \vartheta(1-\beta)\left[\sum_{s=t}^{\infty} D_s P_s (Y_s - G_s) + \sum_{s=t}^{\infty} D_s \frac{i_s}{1+i_s} M_s\right] \qquad (76)$$

$$D_t \frac{i_t}{1+i_t} M_t = \frac{1-\vartheta}{\vartheta} D_t P_t (Y_t - G_t) \qquad (77)$$

Eliminating the quantities of money between (76) and (77), we find that

$$D_t P_t (Y_t - G_t) = (1-\beta)\left[\sum_{s=t}^{\infty} D_s P_s (Y_s - G_s)\right] \qquad (78)$$

Again, financial wealth Ω_t has disappeared, and relation (78) is homogeneous in today's and future prices. We can now compute equilibrium prices. Combining equations (78) above for times t and $t+1$, we obtain a simple recursive equation in nominal prices:

$$D_{t+1} P_{t+1} (Y_{t+1} - G_{t+1}) = \beta D_t P_t (Y_t - G_t) \qquad (79)$$

or

$$\frac{P_{t+1}}{P_t} = \frac{\beta(1+i_t)(Y_t - G_t)}{Y_{t+1} - G_{t+1}} \qquad (80)$$

which generalizes equation (13).

2

Pigou Reconstructed: The Weil Model

2.1 Introduction

We saw in the previous chapter how the distinction between Ricardian and non-Ricardian economies, and whether or not the Pigou effect is present, are important to obtain sensible answers to important questions of monetary theory.

The Ricardian and OLG models that we compared gave extremely opposite results and were quite far apart. It would thus be extremely useful to have a non-Ricardian monetary model that, unlike the OLG model, can "nest" the Ricardian model as a special case. Such a model has been actually developed by Weil (1987, 1991).[1]

So we describe in the next section a simple version of this model that we will use in chapters 3 through 6. We focus in this chapter on how a Pigou effect is generated in such a model and derive some useful dynamic equations.

---

1. The original Weil model is in continuous time and includes money in the utility function (MIUF), whereas the model of this chapter is in discrete time and uses a cash in advance constraint. Nevertheless, these differences are not so important. Appendix A develops a MIUF version of this model in order to show that the fundamental dynamic equation is essentially the same for the two versions.

2.2   The Model

In the Weil model, as in the Sidrauski-Brock Ricardian model, households never die and live an infinite number of periods. But, as in the OLG model, new "generations" of households are born each period. Call N_t the number of households alive at time t. Since no one ever dies, we have $N_{t+1} \geq N_t$. We will mainly work below with the case where the population grows at the constant rate $n \geq 0$ so that $N_t = (1 + n)^t$.

2.2.1   Households

Consider a household j (i.e., a household born in period j). We denote by c_{jt} and m_{jt} his consumption and money holdings at time $t \geq j$. This household receives in periods $t \geq j$ an endowment y_{jt} and maximizes the following utility function:

$$U_{jt} = \sum_{s=t}^{\infty} \beta^{s-t} \log c_{js} \qquad (1)$$

It is submitted in period t to a "cash in advance" constraint

$$P_t c_{jt} \leq m_{jt} \qquad (2)$$

Household j also enters period t with a financial wealth ω_{jt}. Transactions occur in two steps. First the bond market opens, and the household lends an amount b_{jt} at the nominal interest rate i_t (of course, b_{jt} can be negative if the household borrows to obtain liquidity). The rest is kept under the form of money m_{jt} so that

$$\omega_{jt} = m_{jt} + b_{jt} \qquad (3)$$

Then the goods market opens, and the household sells its endowment y_{jt}, pays taxes τ_{jt} in real terms, and consumes c_{jt}, subject to the cash in advance constraint (2). Consequently the budget constraint for household j is

$$\omega_{jt+1} = (1 + i_t)\omega_{jt} - i_t m_{jt} + P_t y_{jt} - P_t \tau_{jt} - P_t c_{jt} \qquad (4)$$

2.2.2 Aggregation

Aggregate quantities are obtained by summing the various individual variables. Since there are $N_j - N_{j-1}$ agents in generation j, these aggregates are equal to

$$Y_t = \sum_{j \leq t}(N_j - N_{j-1})y_{jt}, \quad C_t = \sum_{j \leq t}(N_j - N_{j-1})c_{jt} \tag{5}$$

$$T_t = \sum_{j \leq t}(N_j - N_{j-1})\tau_{jt}, \quad \Omega_t = \sum_{j \leq t}(N_j - N_{j-1})\omega_{jt} \tag{6}$$

$$M_t = \sum_{j \leq t}(N_j - N_{j-1})m_{jt}, \quad B_t = \sum_{j \leq t}(N_j - N_{j-1})b_{jt} \tag{7}$$

2.2.3 Endowments and Taxes

To be complete, we should describe how endowments and taxes are distributed among households. We assume for the time being that all households have the same income and taxes so that

$$y_{jt} = y_t = \frac{Y_t}{N_t}, \quad \tau_{jt} = \tau_t = \frac{T_t}{N_t} \tag{8}$$

A more general scheme will be considered in section 2.6 below. We also assume that endowments per head grow at the rate ζ so that

$$\frac{y_{t+1}}{y_t} = \zeta, \quad \frac{Y_{t+1}}{Y_t} = (1+n)\zeta \tag{9}$$

2.2.4 Government

The households' aggregate financial wealth Ω_t has as a counterpart an identical amount Ω_t of financial liabilities of the government. The evolution of these liabilities is described by the government's budget constraint, which is the same as in chapter 1:

$$\Omega_{t+1} = (1 + i_t)\Omega_t - i_t M_t - P_t T_t \tag{10}$$

2.3   The Dynamics of the Economy

We now derive a number of dynamic relations in this non-Ricardian model. We will see here how and why a Pigou effect develops because of population growth.

2.3.1   Households' Intertemporal Budget Constraints

We will continue to aggregate discounted values with the nominal discount rates:

$$D_t = \prod_{s=0}^{t-1} \frac{1}{1+i_s}, \quad D_0 = 1 \tag{11}$$

Consider the household's budget equation (4). We assume that i_t is strictly positive. Then the household always exactly satisfies the cash-in-advance constraint (2) so that $m_{jt} = P_t c_{jt}$. Thus the budget constraint for period s is written as

$$\omega_{js+1} = (1+i_s)\omega_{js} + P_s y_{js} - P_s \tau_{js} - (1+i_s)P_s c_{js} \tag{12}$$

We apply the discount rate D_{s+1} to this budget constraint to obtain

$$D_{s+1}\omega_{js+1} = D_s \omega_{js} + D_{s+1}(P_s y_{js} - P_s \tau_{js}) - D_s P_s c_{js} \tag{13}$$

If we aggregate all budget constraints (13) from time t to infinity, and assume that $D_s \omega_{js}$ goes to zero as s goes to infinity (the transversality condition), we have the intertemporal budget constraint of the household:

$$\sum_{s=t}^{\infty} D_s P_s c_{js} = D_t \omega_{jt} + \sum_{s=t}^{\infty} D_{s+1} P_s (y_{js} - \tau_{js}) \tag{14}$$

2.3.2   The Consumption Function

Maximizing the utility function (1) subject to the intertemporal budget constraint (14) yields the first-order conditions:

$$D_{s+1}P_{s+1}c_{js+1} = \beta D_s P_s c_{js} \tag{15}$$

Combining these first-order conditions and the intertemporal budget constraint (14) yields the following consumption function for a household j:

$$D_t P_t c_{jt} = (1 - \beta) \left[D_t \omega_{jt} + \sum_{s=t}^{\infty} D_{s+1} P_s (y_{js} - \tau_{js}) \right] \qquad (16)$$

Now insert into (16) the assumption above (equation 8) that $y_{js} = y_s$ and $\tau_{js} = \tau_s$. Summing individual consumption functions (16) across the N_t agents alive in period t, we obtain the aggregate consumption C_t:

$$D_t P_t C_t = (1 - \beta) \left[D_t \Omega_t + N_t \sum_{s=t}^{\infty} D_{s+1} P_s (y_s - \tau_s) \right] \qquad (17)$$

Recall from chapter 1 that the presence of Ω_t in the consumption function at this stage did not necessarily mean that a Pigou effect would arise in the end, because the value of Ω_t was canceled by an identical value of discounted taxes. For this reason we now turn to study the government's budget constraint.

2.3.3 The Government's Intertemporal Budget Constraint

Let us consider the government's budget constraint (10) in period s, multiplied by D_{s+1}:

$$D_{s+1} \Omega_{s+1} = D_s \Omega_s - D_{s+1} P_s T_s - D_{s+1} i_s M_s \qquad (18)$$

Let us define "total taxes" in period s, $\mathcal{T}_s$, as

$$P_s \mathcal{T}_s = P_s T_s + i_s M_s \qquad (19)$$

The total nominal taxes consist of proper taxes $P_s T_s$ and the money economized by the state because of the cash-in-advance constraint $i_s M_s$, the "money tax." By this definition, (18) can be rewritten as

$$D_{s+1} \Omega_{s+1} = D_s \Omega_s - D_{s+1} \mathcal{T}_s \qquad (20)$$

Summing from time t to infinity, and assuming that $D_s \Omega_s$ goes to zero when s goes to infinity, we get

$$D_t \Omega_t = \sum_{s=t}^{\infty} D_{s+1} \mathcal{T}_s \tag{21}$$

We see that as in the Ricardian model every single dollar of financial wealth is matched by discounted current and future taxes. But the difference is that whereas in the Ricardian model the currently alive generation will pay 100 percent of these taxes in the future, in this case some future generations will pay part of the taxes. This will yield a Pigou effect, as the next section demonstrates.

2.4   The Pigou Effect

As we indicated in the introduction, an important part of the story is the Pigou effect, by which financial wealth influences consumption and some dynamic equations. We will show how this effect arises.

2.4.1   Consumption and Financial Assets

Consider the government's budget constraint (18). Replace M_s by $P_s Y_s$ and i_s by $(D_s - D_{s+1})/D_{s+1}$:

$$D_{s+1}\Omega_{s+1} = D_s\Omega_s - (D_s - D_{s+1})P_s Y_s - D_{s+1}P_s T_s \tag{22}$$

Divide by N_s, rewriting this equation as

$$D_{s+1} P_s (y_s - \tau_s) = D_s P_s y_s + \frac{D_{s+1}\Omega_{s+1} - D_s\Omega_s}{N_s} \tag{23}$$

Insert (23) into (17) to obtain

$$D_t P_t C_t = (1 - \beta)\left[N_t \sum_{s=t}^{\infty} D_s P_s y_s + D_t \Omega_t + N_t \sum_{s=t}^{\infty} \frac{D_{s+1}\Omega_{s+1} - D_s\Omega_s}{N_s} \right] \tag{24}$$

which yields, after rearranging the terms in Ω_s,

$$D_t P_t C_t = (1 - \beta) N_t \left[\sum_{s=t}^{\infty} D_s P_s y_s + \sum_{s=t}^{\infty} D_{s+1}\Omega_{s+1}\left(\frac{1}{N_s} - \frac{1}{N_{s+1}} \right) \right] \tag{25}$$

The first sum inside the brackets of (25) is the usual sum of discounted incomes. But we see that as soon as some new generations appear in the future, terms representing nominal wealth appear in the consumption function. This is the Pigou effect (Pigou 1943) or the "real balance effect" (Patinkin 1956). Formula (25) shows in a crystalclear manner how this effect disappears when population is constant.

2.4.2 The Extent of the Pigou Effect

We may wonder what part of financial wealth will be considered "real wealth" by the currently alive generations. Consider the case where by an adequate policy (such a policy will be made explicit in chapter 3) Ω_t remains constant in time and equal to Ω_0. In such a case the "supplementary wealth" beyond discounted incomes is, from (25), equal to

$$\left[\frac{N_t}{D_t}\sum_{s=t}^{\infty} D_{s+1}\left(\frac{1}{N_s}-\frac{1}{N_{s+1}}\right)\right]\Omega_0 = \varpi_t\Omega_0 \qquad (26)$$

It is easy to see that ϖ_t is between 0 and 1, and other things equal, it is larger when the rate of increase of the population is greater. For example, assume that the population's growth rate and the nominal interest rate are constant over time:

$$\frac{N_{t+1}}{N_t} = 1 + n, \qquad i_t = i_0 \qquad (27)$$

Then

$$\varpi_t = \varpi = \frac{n}{n + i_0 + ni_0} \qquad (28)$$

and ϖ_t is increasing in n if $i_0 > 0$.

2.4.3 Taxes and the Pigou Effect

As we have just seen, part of financial assets, now and in the future, represents actual purchasing power in the non-Ricardian model, whereas it does not in the Ricardian model. As we have already hinted at, the reason is the following: some of the future taxes, which are a counterpart of current nominal wealth, will not be paid by the currently alive agents but by future, yet unborn, generations, so this part of Ω_t represents actual purchasing power for the currently alive agents. We will now make this intuition more formal.

From the expression of "total taxes" $\mathcal{T}_s$ in equation (20), the consumption function (24) can be rewritten as

$$D_t P_t C_t = (1 - \beta) \left[N_t \sum_{s=t}^{\infty} D_s P_s y_s + D_t \Omega_t - N_t \sum_{s=t}^{\infty} \frac{D_{s+1} \mathcal{T}_s}{N_s} \right] \quad (29)$$

We see that generations alive in t will pay at time $s > t$ only a fraction $N_t / N_s < 1$ of total taxes. From this the Pigou effect will arise, as we will now see. Combining the two equations (21) and (29), we rewrite the consumption function as

$$D_t P_t C_t = (1 - \beta) \left[N_t \sum_{s=t}^{\infty} D_s P_s y_s + \sum_{s=t}^{\infty} \frac{N_s - N_t}{N_s} D_{s+1} \mathcal{T}_s \right] \quad (30)$$

Note in (30) that $N_s - N_t$ is the number of agents alive in period s but yet unborn at period t. So the wealth of agents currently alive consists of two terms: (1) the discounted sum of their incomes and (2) the part of taxes (including the "money tax") that will be paid by future generations in order to "reimburse" the current financial wealth. The second term is what creates the Pigou effect, and we see that an essential ingredient of it is that there will be future, yet unborn, generations that will share the burden of future taxes that are the counterpart of current financial wealth.

2.5   Intertemporal Equilibrium and a Dynamic Equation

So far we have given a number of equilibrium equations emphasizing the intertemporal structure of the model, notably the intertemporal budget constraints. In the chapters that follow it will be very useful to have a simple dynamic equation relating some central variables at times t and $t + 1$. This is done according to the following proposition:

Proposition 2.1   *The dynamics of the model is characterized by the following dynamic relations:*

$$P_{t+1} Y_{t+1} = \beta \frac{N_{t+1}}{N_t} (1 + i_t) P_t Y_t - (1 - \beta) \left(\frac{N_{t+1}}{N_t} - 1 \right) \Omega_{t+1} \qquad (31)$$

or if $N_{t+1}/N_t = 1 + n$,

$$P_{t+1} Y_{t+1} = \beta(1 + n)(1 + i_t) P_t Y_t - (1 - \beta)n\Omega_{t+1} \qquad (32)$$

Proof   Insert the condition $C_t = Y_t$ into (25) and divide by N_t:

$$D_t P_t y_t = (1 - \beta) \left[\sum_{s=t}^{\infty} D_s P_s y_s + \sum_{s=t}^{\infty} D_{s+1} \Omega_{s+1} \left(\frac{1}{N_s} - \frac{1}{N_{s+1}} \right) \right] \qquad (33)$$

We next rewrite (33) for $t + 1$:

$$D_{t+1} P_{t+1} y_{t+1}$$

$$= (1 - \beta) \left[\sum_{s=t+1}^{\infty} D_s P_s y_s + \sum_{s=t+1}^{\infty} D_{s+1} \Omega_{s+1} \left(\frac{1}{N_s} - \frac{1}{N_{s+1}} \right) \right] \qquad (34)$$

Subtract (33) from (34):

$$D_{t+1} P_{t+1} y_{t+1} = \beta D_t P_t y_t - (1 - \beta) \left(\frac{1}{N_t} - \frac{1}{N_{t+1}} \right) D_{t+1} \Omega_{t+1} \qquad (35)$$

Multiplying by N_{t+1}/D_{t+1}, we obtain (31). Replacing N_{t+1}/N_t by $1 + n$ we obtain (32). ∎

Note that equations (31) and (32) strongly resemble traditional Euler equations. The big difference is the presence of the last terms in equations (31) and (32), which introduce nominal wealth and are a consequence of the Pigou effect. As we will see in the next chapters, this creates a number of striking and actually more intuitive results.

2.6   A Generalization: Decreasing Resources

To simplify the exposition we have made so far the particular assumption that agents in all generations have exactly the same endowment and taxes (equation 8), and this is an assumption that we will keep for simplicity in many developments that follow. Nevertheless, in order to explain within this model some properties of the OLG model in the first chapter, like price determinacy or liquidity effects (these will be studied in chapter 3 to 6), it will be useful to make a simple further generalization. Namely we will assume that relative endowments and taxes decrease with age as follows:

$$y_{jt} = \psi^{t-j} y_t, \quad \tau_{jt} = \psi^{t-j} \tau_t, \qquad \psi \leq 1, \, j \leq t \tag{36}$$

where y_t and τ_t are the income and taxes of a newborn agent in period t. The assumption in equation (8) corresponds to $\psi = 1$.

Under the more general hypothesis (36) proposition 2.1 is replaced by

Proposition 2.2 *Assume that the population grows at the rate $n > 0$. Under hypothesis (36) the dynamics of the model are characterized by the following relation:*

$$\psi P_{t+1} Y_{t+1} = \beta(1+n)(1+i_t) P_t Y_t - (1-\beta)(1+n-\psi)\Omega_{t+1} \tag{37}$$

Proof   See appendix C.   ∎

2.7   The Autarkic Interest Rate

In this book we are essentially interested in equilibria (and dynamic paths) where financial assets are positively valued and create an operative link between the various generations. But, since Samuelson (1958) and Gale (1973) we know that in OLG models there are also equilibria where each generation somehow lives in an "autarky." It will become evident in subsequent chapters that a similar phenomenon appears in this model for some equilibria. Moreover the real interest rate that prevails in such "autarkic" equilibria will be shown to play an important role in the determinacy conditions that we will obtain in chapters 4 to 6, so it is useful to characterize it now.

We begin with the more general model of section 2.6. Recall the utility functions

$$U_{jt} = \sum_{s=t}^{\infty} \beta^{s-t} \log c_{js} \tag{38}$$

and the endowments

$$y_{jt} = \psi^{t-j} y_t \qquad (39)$$

$$y_{t+1} = \zeta y_t \qquad (40)$$

To make things simple, assume that government spending and taxes are zero so that the assumption that we are in autarkic equilibrium translates into

$$c_{jt} = y_{jt} \qquad \forall j, t \qquad (41)$$

Maximization of utility under the intertemporal budget constraint yields the first-order condition:

$$P_{t+1} c_{jt+1} = \beta(1 + i_t) P_t c_{jt} \qquad (42)$$

Recall the definition of the gross real interest rate R_t,

$$R_t = 1 + r_t = \frac{(1 + i_t) P_t}{P_{t+1}} \qquad (43)$$

We can define the autarkic interest rate as the real rate of interest that will prevail under an "autarkic" situation characterized by equalities (41). We then have:

Proposition 2.3 *Under hypotheses* (39) *and* (40) *the autarkic gross real interest rate, which we denote as ξ, is equal to*

$$\xi = \frac{\psi \zeta}{\beta} \qquad (44)$$

Proof Combining equations (39) to (43), we obtain (44). ∎

Note that the quantity $\psi \zeta$ in the numerator of (44) is the rate of increase of individual endowments since, combining (39) and (40), we obtain

$$y_{jt+1} = \psi \zeta y_{jt} \qquad (45)$$

We will see in the next chapters that this autarkic interest rate ξ will play a central role in a number of determinacy conditions.

2.8   Conclusions

We described in this chapter a model of Weil (1987, 1991), that is somehow an intermediate between the Ricardian and the OLG models. As in the Ricardian model all agents are infinitely lived, but as in the OLG model new agents enter the economy over time. The Ricardian model appears as a particular limit case where the rate of birth is zero. We saw that a Pigou effect naturally appears in this model (Weil 1991). The reason is that in a model with a single family of agents, every single cent of financial wealth today is compensated by the same amount of discounted taxes in the future. As a result it does not represent any real wealth now, as we already saw in chapter 1. In the non-Ricardian economy, part of these future taxes will be paid by yet unborn agents, and this part that will be paid by unborn agents represents real wealth to currently alive agents (equation 30).

   We will see in the next chapters that this feature brings major changes in the study of many important monetary issues.

2.9   References

The model in this chapter is due to Weil (1987, 1991), who showed notably that financial assets are net wealth in these models (the Pigou effect).

   The first model with a demographic structure similar to that in this chapter is due to Blanchard (1985). The emphasis was put on the stochastic death rate of households, which could be handled elegantly using a life insurance scheme due to Yaari (1965).

   Later Weil (1989) showed that the important results in such models could be obtained in a model with only births and no deaths. This result was confirmed by Buiter (1988), who built a model with different rates of death and birth. In particular, if there is no birth but a constant rate of death, Ricardian equivalence still prevails. So, since the important non-Ricardian results are due to the birth rate and not to the death rate, we use for simplicity a model with birth only.

   The structure of long-term equilibria in OLG models was notably studied by Gale (1973).

Appendix A: Money in the Utility Function

Instead of using the cash-in-advance specification, we shall now use a money in the utility function formulation, as in appendix B of chapter 1. However, this time the model used is the non-Ricardian model developed in this chapter.

The Model

Again, assume that N_t households are alive at time t. All households have the same endowment and taxes per capita:

$$y_{jt} = y_t = \frac{Y_t}{N_t}, \quad \tau_t = \tau_t = \frac{T_t}{N_t} \tag{46}$$

A household born in period j maximizes the following utility function in period $t \geq j$:

$$U_{jt} = \sum_{s=t}^{\infty} \beta^{s-t} \left[\vartheta \log c_{js} + (1 - \vartheta) \log \frac{m_{js}}{P_s} \right] \tag{47}$$

Household j enters period t with a financial wealth ω_{jt}. It sells its endowment y_t, pays taxes τ_t in real terms, and consumes c_{jt}. What is left is allocated between money m_{jt} and bonds b_{jt} according to the budget constraint

$$m_{jt} + b_{jt} = \omega_{jt} + P_t y_t - P_t \tau_t - P_t c_{jt} \tag{48}$$

Financial wealth next period ω_{jt+1} is given by

$$\omega_{jt+1} = (1 + i_t) b_{jt} + m_{jt} \tag{49}$$

Combining these two relations, we obtain the equation giving the evolution of household j's financial wealth between two successive periods:

$$\omega_{jt+1} = (1 + i_t) \left(\omega_{jt} + P_t y_t - P_t \tau_t - P_t c_{jt} - \frac{i_t}{1 + i_t} m_{jt} \right) \tag{50}$$

Aggregate quantities are simply obtained by aggregating the various individual variables. The total financial liabilities of the government Ω_t evolve according to

$$\Omega_{t+1} = (1 + i_t)\left(\Omega_t - P_t T_t - \frac{i_t}{1 + i_t} M_t\right) \tag{51}$$

The Dynamic Equation

Consider the N_t households alive in period t. By the same method as in section 2.3, we find that the consumption function and demand for money of each particular agent j have the same form as seen in appendix B of chapter 1:

$$D_t P_t c_{jt} = \vartheta(1 - \beta)\left[D_t \omega_{jt} + \sum_{s=t}^{\infty} D_s P_s(y_s - \tau_s)\right] \tag{52}$$

$$D_t \frac{i_t}{1 + i_t} m_{jt} = (1 - \vartheta)(1 - \beta)\left[D_t \omega_{jt} + \sum_{s=t}^{\infty} D_s P_s(y_s - \tau_s)\right] \tag{53}$$

Because the propensities to consume are the same across all agents, these individual functions for the N_t individuals alive in period t aggregate easily as

$$D_t P_t C_t = \vartheta(1 - \beta)\left[D_t \Omega_t + N_t \sum_{s=t}^{\infty} D_s P_s(y_s - \tau_s)\right] \tag{54}$$

$$D_t \frac{i_t}{1 + i_t} M_t = (1 - \vartheta)(1 - \beta)\left[D_t \Omega_t + N_t \sum_{s=t}^{\infty} D_s P_s(y_s - \tau_s)\right] \tag{55}$$

Let us add to the aggregate relations above the condition for equilibrium on the goods market:

$$C_t = Y_t = N_t y_t \tag{56}$$

In accord with (56), equations (54) and (55) become

$$D_t P_t y_t = \vartheta(1 - \beta)\left[\frac{D_t \Omega_t}{N_t} + \sum_{s=t}^{\infty} D_s P_s(y_s - \tau_s)\right] \tag{57}$$

$$D_t \frac{i_t}{1 + i_t} M_t = \frac{1 - \vartheta}{\vartheta} D_t P_t N_t y_t \tag{58}$$

If we forward equation (57) one period, we have

$$D_{t+1} P_{t+1} y_{t+1} = \vartheta(1 - \beta)\left[\frac{D_{t+1}\Omega_{t+1}}{N_{t+1}} + \sum_{s=t+1}^{\infty} D_s P_s(y_s - \tau_s)\right] \tag{59}$$

Then, subtracting (57) from (59):

$$D_{t+1} P_{t+1} y_{t+1} - D_t P_t y_t$$

$$= \vartheta(1 - \beta)\left[\frac{D_{t+1}\Omega_{t+1}}{N_{t+1}} - \frac{D_t \Omega_t}{N_t} + D_t P_t(y_t - \tau_t)\right] \tag{60}$$

Multiplying the government budget constraint (51) by D_{t+1}/N_t gives us

$$\frac{D_{t+1}\Omega_{t+1}}{N_t} = \frac{D_t \Omega_t}{N_t} - D_t P_t \tau_t - \frac{1}{N_t} D_t \frac{i_t}{1 + i_t} M_t \tag{61}$$

Using (58), we write

$$\frac{D_{t+1}\Omega_{t+1}}{N_t} = \frac{D_t \Omega_t}{N_t} - D_t P_t \tau_t - \frac{1 - \vartheta}{\vartheta} D_t P_t y_t \tag{62}$$

After inserting (62) into (60), we have

$$D_{t+1} P_{t+1} y_{t+1} - \beta D_t P_t y_t = \vartheta(1 - \beta)\left[\frac{D_{t+1}\Omega_{t+1}}{N_{t+1}} - \frac{D_{t+1}\Omega_{t+1}}{N_t}\right] \tag{63}$$

Then multiplied by N_{t+1}/D_{t+1}, this yields the dynamic equation

$$P_{t+1} Y_{t+1} = \beta \frac{N_{t+1}}{N_t}(1 + i_t)P_t Y_t - \vartheta(1 - \beta)\left(\frac{N_{t+1}}{N_t} - 1\right)\Omega_{t+1} \tag{64}$$

which is very similar to equation (31).

Appendix B: Existence Conditions

We explore in this appendix a few sufficient conditions for the existence of an intertemporal equilibrium.[2] There are two sets of conditions.

Transversality Conditions

The first condition comes from the transversality condition of a household's maximization problem. It basically says that the discounted value of household j's assets $D_t \omega_{jt}$ should go to zero as time goes to infinity. Let us recall equation (13) giving the evolution of these assets:

$$D_{t+1} \omega_{jt+1} = D_t \omega_{jt} + D_{t+1}(P_t y_t - P_t \tau_t) - D_t P_t c_{jt} \tag{65}$$

and equation (16) giving individual consumption:

$$D_t P_t c_{jt} = (1 - \beta) \left[D_t \omega_{jt} + \sum_{s=t}^{\infty} D_{s+1} P_s (y_s - \tau_s) \right] \tag{66}$$

Combining the two, we obtain

$$D_{t+1} \omega_{jt+1} = \beta D_t \omega_{jt} + D_{t+1} P_t (y_t - \tau_t) - (1 - \beta) \sum_{s=t}^{\infty} D_{s+1} P_s (y_s - \tau_s) \tag{67}$$

Now combining equation (17) giving aggregate consumption with the equality $C_t = Y_t$ we obtain, after dividing by N_t:

$$D_t P_t y_t = (1 - \beta) \left[\frac{D_t \Omega_t}{N_t} + \sum_{s=t}^{\infty} D_{s+1} P_s (y_s - \tau_s) \right] \tag{68}$$

Inserting (68) into (67) gives

$$D_{t+1} \omega_{jt+1} = \beta D_t \omega_{jt} + (1 - \beta) \frac{D_t \Omega_t}{N_t} + D_{t+1} P_t (y_t - \tau_t) - D_t P_t y_t \tag{69}$$

2. These conditions were studied by Weil (1987, 1991) for the continuous time version of the model with money in the utility function and isoelastic utility functions.

Now let us recall the government's budget constraint (23):

$$D_{t+1}P_t(y_t - \tau_t) = D_t P_t y_t + \frac{D_{t+1}\Omega_{t+1} - D_t\Omega_t}{N_t} \tag{70}$$

Inserting (70) into (69), we finally have

$$D_{t+1}\omega_{jt+1} = \beta D_t \omega_{jt} + \frac{D_{t+1}\Omega_{t+1}}{N_t} - \beta\frac{D_t\Omega_t}{N_t} \tag{71}$$

Clearly, if $D_t\Omega_t/N_t$ goes to zero, the transversality condition will be satisfied.

The Feasibility of Individual Consumptions

The second feasibility condition can actually take two forms. The first form corresponds to the condition that the rates of growth of individual consumptions cannot be greater than the rate of growth of global resources. To find the individual rate of consumption growth, we recall the maximization program of household j:

$$\text{Max} \sum_{s=t}^{\infty} \beta^{s-t} \log c_{js} \quad \text{s.t.}$$

$$\sum_{s=t}^{\infty} D_s P_s c_{js} = D_t \omega_{jt} + \sum_{s=t}^{\infty} D_{s+1} P_s (y_s - \tau_s)$$

The corresponding Euler equation is

$$P_{t+1}c_{jt+1} = \beta(1 + i_t)P_t c_{jt} \tag{72}$$

This means that the rate of growth of individual consumption c_{jt} is

$$\frac{c_{jt+1}}{c_{jt}} = \frac{\beta(1 + i_t)P_t}{P_{t+1}} \tag{73}$$

which, to be feasible, must be smaller than the rate of growth of global resources $\zeta(1 + n)$. In steady state $i_t = i_0$ and

$$\frac{P_{t+1}}{P_t} = \frac{\Omega_{t+1}}{\Omega_t} \frac{1}{\zeta(1+n)} \tag{74}$$

So this condition becomes

$$\frac{\Omega_{t+1}}{\Omega_t} \geq \beta(1 + i_0) \tag{75}$$

A second way to assess the feasibility of individual consumptions is to look at the consumption function of generation j (equation 66):

$$D_t P_t c_{jt} = (1 - \beta) \left[D_t \omega_{jt} + \sum_{s=t}^{\infty} D_{s+1} P_s (y_s - \tau_s) \right] \tag{76}$$

Note that a necessary condition for all generations, and notably for the newborn generation who has no initial assets, to have a positive consumption is

$$\sum_{s=t}^{\infty} D_{s+1} P_s (y_s - \tau_s) \geq 0 \tag{77}$$

Combine (17) with $Y_t = C_t$. This yields the aggregate equilibrium condition:

$$D_t P_t Y_t = (1 - \beta) \left[D_t \Omega_t + N_t \sum_{s=t}^{\infty} D_{s+1} P_s (y_s - \tau_s) \right] \tag{78}$$

Then, combining (77) and (78), we obtain the following condition:

$$P_t Y_t \geq (1 - \beta)\Omega_t \tag{79}$$

Although conditions (75) and (79) may look different, they actually lead to the same condition on economic policy. To see this, let us assume that "total taxes" (equation 19) are a constant fraction of financial wealth:

$$P_t T_t = P_t T_t + i_t M_t = \chi \Omega_t \tag{80}$$

Inserting this into the government budget constraint yields

$$\Omega_{t+1} = (1 + i_0 - \chi)\Omega_t \tag{81}$$

We can combine (81) with (75) to get

$$\chi < (1 - \beta)(1 + i_0) \tag{82}$$

Note, in particular, that if $\chi = 0$, this condition will be satisfied for any value of the interest rate. So, in general fiscal policy must not be too deflationary.

Let us move to condition (79). Recall the dynamic equation

$$P_{t+1}Y_{t+1} = \beta(1 + n)(1 + i_0)P_tY_t - (1 - \beta)n\Omega_{t+1} \tag{83}$$

Under policy (80) we have

$$\frac{P_{t+1}Y_{t+1}}{P_tY_t} = \frac{\Omega_{t+1}}{\Omega_t} = 1 + i_0 - \chi \tag{84}$$

Combining (83) and (84) yields

$$\frac{\Omega_t}{P_tY_t} = \frac{\beta(1 + n)(1 + i_0) - (1 + i_0 - \chi)}{(1 - \beta)n(1 + i_0 - \chi)} \tag{85}$$

which, combined with (79), gives the following condition on policy:

$$\chi < (1 - \beta)(1 + i_0) \tag{86}$$

This is indeed exactly the same constraint as (82).

Appendix C: Proof of Proposition 2.2

The derivation of the consumption function for generation j is essentially the same as for $\psi = 1$, except for the fact that we must take into account the fact that income y_{jt} and taxes τ_{jt} now explicitly depend on the date j the household was born. So the consumption function of generation j is, after combining (16) and (36),

$$D_t P_t c_{jt} = (1 - \beta) \left[D_t \omega_{jt} + \sum_{s=t}^{\infty} D_{s+1} P_s (y_{js} - \tau_{js}) \right]$$

$$= (1 - \beta) \left[D_t \omega_{jt} + \sum_{s=t}^{\infty} D_{s+1} P_s \psi^{s-j} (y_s - \tau_s) \right] \qquad (87)$$

There are $N_j - N_{j-1}$ households in generation j. So, summing over all generations $j \leq t$, we obtain total consumption C_t:

$$D_t P_t C_t = (1 - \beta) \left[D_t \Omega_t + \sum_{j=-\infty}^{t} (N_j - N_{j-1}) \sum_{s=t}^{\infty} D_{s+1} P_s \psi^{s-j} (y_s - \tau_s) \right]$$

$$= (1 - \beta) \left[D_t \Omega_t + \sum_{j=-\infty}^{t} \psi^{t-j} (N_j - N_{j-1}) \sum_{s=t}^{\infty} D_{s+1} P_s \psi^{s-t} (y_s - \tau_s) \right]$$

$$\qquad (88)$$

Now let us define

$$\mathcal{N}_t = \sum_{j=-\infty}^{t} \psi^{t-j} (N_j - N_{j-1}) \qquad (89)$$

If $N_t = (1 + n)^t$, $n > 0$, then

$$\mathcal{N}_t = \frac{n N_t}{1 + n - \psi} \qquad (90)$$

We have

$$y_t = \frac{Y_t}{\mathcal{N}_t} \quad \tau_t = \frac{T_t}{\mathcal{N}_t} \qquad (91)$$

Aggregate consumption (equation 88) is therefore now given by

$$D_t P_t C_t = (1 - \beta) \left[D_t \Omega_t + \mathcal{N}_t \sum_{s=t}^{\infty} D_{s+1} P_s \psi^{s-t} (y_s - \tau_s) \right] \qquad (92)$$

The equilibrium equation is obtained by inserting $C_t = Y_t$ into (92):

$$D_t P_t Y_t = (1 - \beta) \left[D_t \Omega_t + \mathcal{N}_t \sum_{s=t}^{\infty} D_{s+1} P_s \psi^{s-t}(y_s - \tau_s) \right] \quad (93)$$

Divide both sides by $\mathcal{N}_t$ and use $Y_t = \mathcal{N}_t y_t$:

$$D_t P_t y_t = (1 - \beta) \left[\frac{D_t \Omega_t}{\mathcal{N}_t} + \sum_{s=t}^{\infty} D_{s+1} P_s \psi^{s-t}(y_s - \tau_s) \right] \quad (94)$$

Let us rewrite this equation for $t + 1$:

$$D_{t+1} P_{t+1} y_{t+1} = (1 - \beta) \left[\frac{D_{t+1} \Omega_{t+1}}{\mathcal{N}_{t+1}} + \sum_{s=t+1}^{\infty} D_{s+1} P_s \psi^{s-t-1}(y_s - \tau_s) \right] \quad (95)$$

Let us now multiply (95) by ψ and subtract (94) from it:

$$\psi D_{t+1} P_{t+1} y_{t+1} - D_t P_t y_t$$

$$= (1 - \beta) \left[\frac{\psi D_{t+1} \Omega_{t+1}}{\mathcal{N}_{t+1}} - \frac{D_t \Omega_t}{\mathcal{N}_t} - D_{t+1} P_t (y_t - \tau_t) \right] \quad (96)$$

Multiply the government's budget equation (10) by $D_{t+1}/\mathcal{N}_t$:

$$\frac{D_t \Omega_t}{\mathcal{N}_t} = \frac{D_{t+1} \Omega_{t+1}}{\mathcal{N}_t} + D_{t+1} P_t \tau_t + (D_t - D_{t+1}) P_t y_t \quad (97)$$

Insert (97) into (96):

$$\psi D_{t+1} P_{t+1} y_{t+1} = \beta D_t P_t y_t + (1 - \beta) \left(\frac{\psi}{\mathcal{N}_{t+1}} - \frac{1}{\mathcal{N}_t} \right) D_{t+1} \Omega_{t+1} \quad (98)$$

Multiply (98) by $\mathcal{N}_{t+1}/D_{t+1}$:

$$\psi P_{t+1} Y_{t+1} = \beta \frac{\mathcal{N}_{t+1}}{\mathcal{N}_t} (1 + i_t) P_t Y_t - (1 - \beta) \left(\frac{\mathcal{N}_{t+1}}{\mathcal{N}_t} - \psi \right) \Omega_{t+1} \quad (99)$$

Taking finally from (90) $\mathcal{N}_{t+1}/\mathcal{N}_t = N_{t+1}/N_t = 1 + n$, we obtain

$$\psi P_{t+1} Y_{t+1} = \beta(1 + n)(1 + i_t)P_t Y_t - (1 - \beta)(1 + n - \psi)\Omega_{t+1} \qquad (100)$$

which is equation (37).

Part II

Interest, Prices, and Money

3

Liquidity Effects

3.1 Introduction

We begin our investigation of monetary issues in non-Ricardian models
with the problem of liquidity effects in dynamic stochastic general equilibrium (DSGE) models. As we saw in chapter 1, this liquidity effect, which
is a negative response of the nominal interest rate to monetary injections,
is difficult to obtain in the Ricardian monetary DSGE models. The
reason is the inflationary expectations effect, also described formally in
chapter 1, and which raises the nominal interest rate in response to a
monetary injection.

In this chapter we show that a liquidity effect naturally occurs in a non-
Ricardian environment. The line of reasoning is as follows: as we have
seen, in a non-Ricardian economy a Pigou effect is present. And this
Pigou effect produces a liquidity effect, as we will demonstrate formally
below. But before developing a fully rigorous model, we will give a brief
intuitive argument based on the traditional IS-LM model.

3.2 Liquidity Effects in a Simple IS-LM Model

To guide our intuition as to why the Pigou effect leads to a liquidity
effect, we take a simple traditional IS-LM model augmented with such a

Pigou effect. To make the exposition particularly simple, we write this model in loglinear form:

$$y = -a(i - \pi^e) + b(\omega - p) + cy \qquad \text{IS} \qquad (1)$$

$$m - p = -di + ey \qquad\qquad \text{LM} \qquad (2)$$

$$y = y_0 \qquad\qquad\qquad\qquad (3)$$

where π^e is the expected rate of inflation, $\omega = \log \Omega$, $p = \log P$ and

$$a > 0, \quad b > 0, \quad c > 0, \quad d > 0, \quad e > 0 \qquad (4)$$

Equation (3) gives the market-clearing hypothesis (which will be assumed throughout this chapter). The IS equation (1) says that output is equal to demand, which itself depends negatively on the real interest rate $i - \pi^e$, and positively on real wealth $\omega - p$. Note that the presence of this last term with $b > 0$, which corresponds to a Pigou effect, is specific of the non-Ricardian framework. We can solve for the nominal interest rate i and price level p. Omitting irrelevant constants this yields

$$i = \frac{a\pi^e - bm}{a + bd} \qquad (5)$$

$$p = \frac{ad\pi^e + am}{a + bd} \qquad (6)$$

Then differentiating the expression of i in (5) yields

$$\frac{\partial i}{\partial m} = \frac{1}{a + bd}\left(a\frac{\partial \pi^e}{\partial m} - b\right) \qquad (7)$$

We recognize two effects: The first term in the parenthesis corresponds to the "inflationary expectations effect," which is positive if a positive money shock raises inflationary expectations ($\partial \pi^e/\partial m > 0$). Then there is a negative "liquidity effect" due to the Pigou effect ($b > 0$).

Now the underlying mechanism for the liquidity effect is the following: an increase in money creates a price increase (equation 6). This price increase decreases demand because of the Pigou effect (the second term in the right-hand side of equation 1). To maintain total demand at the market-clearing level, the first term in (1) must increase, meaning that the real rate of interest must decrease. This decrease in the real interest rate creates the liquidity effect.

3.3 The Model and Monetary Policy

We now develop the argument above in the framework of a rigorous non-Ricardian model. We will use the Weil model, already described in chapter 2, section 2.2. We must now be a little more specific about monetary policy.

3.3.1 Monetary Policy

There are several ways to model monetary policy, that is, how government intervenes on the bonds market. For example, the government can target the quantity of money, the interest rate, or any intermediate objective. In this chapter, as in all studies on the liquidity effect, we will assume that the government uses the quantity of money M_t as the policy variable, and that consequently the nominal interest rate i_t is endogenously determined through the equilibrium in the bonds market.

Let us recall that at the beginning of period t agents go to the bonds market and allocate their aggregate financial wealth Ω_t between money and bonds:

$$M_t + B_t = \Omega_t \tag{8}$$

The government aims at choosing directly the value of M_t. A positive shock on money M_t corresponds to a purchase of bonds (against money) by the government. Following the literature, we will make the assumption that M_t is a stochastic process. For example, it is often assumed that money increases are autocorrelated over time:

$$\log\left(\frac{M_t}{M_{t-1}}\right) = \frac{\varepsilon_t}{1 - \rho\mathcal{L}}, \qquad 0 \leq \rho < 1 \tag{9}$$

where ε_t is an i.i.d. stochastic variable and $\mathcal{L}$ is the lag operator.

As indicated above, we will say there is a liquidity effect if a positive shock on M_t leads to a decrease in i_t.

3.4   Dynamic Equilibrium

We now derive the dynamics of the model. The central equation, which describes the dynamics of nominal income, turns out to be a stochastic version of equation (32) in chapter 2:

Proposition 3.1   *The dynamics of nominal income is given by*

$$E_t(P_{t+1} Y_{t+1}) = \beta(1 + n)(1 + i_t)P_t Y_t - (1 - \beta)n\Omega_{t+1} \qquad (10)$$

Proof   See the appendix at the end of this chapter.   ■

Because the model is non-Ricardian, the complete dynamics will depend on the actual tax policy. Let us recall the equation of evolution of Ω_t:

$$\Omega_{t+1} = (1 + i_t)\Omega_t - i_t M_t - P_t T_t \qquad (11)$$

Because our emphasis is on monetary policy, and in order to simplify the dynamics below, we will choose the simplest tax policy, and assume that the government balances its budget period by period. Taxes will thus cover exactly interest payments on bonds:

$$P_t T_t = i_t B_t \qquad (12)$$

We can immediately note, based on (8) and (11), that under the balanced budget policy (12) total financial wealth will remain constant:

$$\Omega_t = \Omega_0 \qquad \text{for all } t \qquad (13)$$

The dynamic equation (10) then becomes

$$E_t(P_{t+1} Y_{t+1}) = \beta(1 + n)(1 + i_t)P_t Y_t - (1 - \beta)n\Omega_0 \qquad (14)$$

Since $M_t = P_t C_t = P_t Y_t$, equation (14) can be rewritten as

$$E_t M_{t+1} = \beta(1 + n)(1 + i_t)M_t - (1 - \beta)n\Omega_0 \qquad (15)$$

3.5 Liquidity Effects

We will now see that the non-Ricardian character of the economy, that is, the fact that $n > 0$, will produce a liquidity effect.

3.5.1 The Nominal Interest Rate

We can actually solve explicitly equation (15) for the nominal interest rate

$$1 + i_t = \frac{1}{\beta(1+n)} E_t\left(\frac{M_{t+1}}{M_t}\right) + \frac{(1-\beta)n\Omega_0}{\beta(1+n)M_t} \qquad (16)$$

Note that the first term, which is present even if $n = 0$, displays the "inflationary expectations effect." The nominal interest rate will rise if a positive monetary shock announces future money growth, that is, if

$$\frac{\partial}{\partial M_t}\left[E_t\left(\frac{M_{t+1}}{M_t}\right)\right] > 0 \qquad (17)$$

which is what is generally found empirically. In the example above (equation 9) this will occur if $\rho > 0$. We can assume in what follows that the money process satisfies condition (17).

Now the second term, which appears only if $n > 0$, meaning if we are in a non-Ricardian framework, clearly introduces a liquidity effect, since an increase in money directly decreases the nominal interest rate. The higher n, the stronger is this effect.

We can give an even simpler expression. Assume that money M_t is stationary around the value M_0. From (15) the corresponding stationary value of the interest rate, i_0, is related to M_0 and Ω_0 by

$$M_0 = \beta(1+n)(1+i_0)M_0 - (1-\beta)n\Omega_0 \qquad (18)$$

Let us define the composite parameter

$$\theta = \beta(1+n)(1+i_0) \qquad (19)$$

If we want to have a Pigou effect, net financial assets must be positive, meaning $\Omega_0 > 0$. As a consequence from (18) the parameter θ must satisfy

$$\theta > 1 \tag{20}$$

Now combining (16), (18), and (19), we obtain

$$\frac{1 + i_t}{1 + i_0} = \frac{1}{\theta} E_t \left(\frac{M_{t+1}}{M_t} \right) + \left(1 - \frac{1}{\theta} \right) \frac{M_0}{M_t} \tag{21}$$

We see that formula (21) gives a balanced view between the new non-Ricardian liquidity effect and the traditional inflationary expectations effect. We can note that the higher θ (and thus notably the higher n), the stronger will be the liquidity effect.

3.5.2   The Real Interest Rate

Recall the definition of the gross real interest rate R_t:

$$R_t = 1 + r_t = (1 + i_t) \frac{P_t}{P_{t+1}} \tag{22}$$

Now $Y_{t+1}/Y_t = (1 + n)\zeta$. Combining this with $M_t = P_t Y_t$, and equations (18), (19), and (21), we obtain

$$\frac{1}{R_t} = \frac{\beta}{\zeta} \frac{M_{t+1}/M_t}{E_t(M_{t+1}/M_t) + (\theta - 1)(M_0/M_t)} \tag{23}$$

and

$$E_t \left(\frac{1}{R_t} \right) = \frac{\beta}{\zeta} \frac{E_t(M_{t+1}/M_t)}{E_t(M_{t+1}/M_t) + (\theta - 1)(M_0/M_t)} \tag{24}$$

In view of assumption (17) we see that the real interest rate will react negatively to a positive money shock, in the sense that

$$\frac{\partial}{\partial M_t} \left[E_t \left(\frac{1}{R_t} \right) \right] > 0 \tag{25}$$

This real interest rate effect will counteract the inflationary expectations effect, and is at the basis of the liquidity effect.

3.6   A Stronger Liquidity Effect

We shall now see that the liquidity effect is strengthened in the more general case seen in chapter 2, section 2.6, where households' resources evolve over time as follows:

$$y_{jt} = \psi^{t-j} y_t, \quad \tau_{jt} = \psi^{t-j} \tau_t, \qquad \psi \le 1 \tag{26}$$

where y_t and τ_t are the income and taxes of a newborn agent in period t. We have the following proposition, which generalizes proposition 3.1:

Proposition 3.2 *Consider a non-Ricardian economy $(n > 0)$ where endowments and taxes evolve according to* (26). *Then the dynamics of nominal income is given by*

$$\psi E_t(P_{t+1} Y_{t+1}) = \beta(1 + n)(1 + i_t) P_t Y_t - (1 - \beta)(1 + n - \psi)\Omega_{t+1} \tag{27}$$

Proof   See the appendix at the end of the chapter.   ■

If we use $M_t = P_t C_t = P_t Y_t$ and the fact that under fiscal policy (12), $\Omega_t = \Omega_0$ for all t, equation (27) becomes

$$\psi E_t M_{t+1} = \beta(1 + n)(1 + i_t) M_t - (1 - \beta)(1 + n - \psi)\Omega_0 \tag{28}$$

We solve for the nominal interest rate

$$1 + i_t = \frac{\psi}{\beta(1 + n)} E_t\left(\frac{M_{t+1}}{M_t}\right) + \frac{(1 - \beta)(1 + n - \psi)\Omega_0}{\beta(1 + n) M_t} \tag{29}$$

in which we see that the second term does produce a liquidity effect. Now from (28) the stationary values of M_0, Ω_0 and i_0 are related by

$$\psi M_0 = \beta(1 + n)(1 + i_0) M_0 - (1 - \beta)(1 + n - \psi)\Omega_0 \tag{30}$$

Let us now give a more general definition of the parameter θ:

$$\theta = \frac{\beta(1 + n)(1 + i_0)}{\psi} \tag{31}$$

By combining (29), (30), and (31), we find that the nominal interest rate is given by

$$\frac{1+i_t}{1+i_0} = \frac{1}{\theta}E_t\left(\frac{M_{t+1}}{M_t}\right) + \left(1 - \frac{1}{\theta}\right)\frac{M_0}{M_t} \tag{32}$$

This is exactly the same expression as (21), but the expression of θ has been generalized from (19) to (31). We see that a lower value of ψ increases the value of θ and therefore enhances the non-Ricardian liquidity effect. In the extreme case where $\psi = 0$ (i.e., when agents have all their income in the first period of their life), θ is infinite and the liquidity effect totally dominates.

Note that the result above gives us an explanation of why the liquidity effect always dominated in the OLG model in chapter 1. Recall that households in that model have no resources in the second period, which makes that OLG model similar to the model of this section with $\psi = 0$. This is precisely the case where, as we just saw, the liquidity effect fully dominates.

3.7   The Persistence of the Liquidity Effect

We will now show that we have not only a liquidity effect but that this effect can be quite persistent. Let us loglinearize equations (21) or (32), which yields

$$\frac{i_t - i_0}{1 + i_0} = \frac{1}{\theta}(E_t m_{t+1} - m_t) - \left(1 - \frac{1}{\theta}\right)(m_t - m_0) \tag{33}$$

where the Ricardian particular case is obtained by taking $\theta = 1$. We consider the following stationary money process:

$$m_t - m_0 = \frac{\varepsilon_t}{(1 - \rho\mathcal{L})(1 - \mu\mathcal{L})}, \qquad 0 < \rho < 1, \, 0 < \mu < 1 \tag{34}$$

where ε_t is i.i.d. Then

$$E_t m_{t+1} - m_t = \frac{(\mu + \rho - 1 - \mu\rho\mathcal{L})\varepsilon_t}{(1 - \rho\mathcal{L})(1 - \mu\mathcal{L})} \tag{35}$$

If $\mu + \rho > 1$, a positive monetary innovation $\varepsilon_t > 0$ creates the expectation of a monetary increase next period, which is the assumption traditionally associated with the "inflationary expectations effect" (equation 17). We will assume $\mu + \rho > 1$ so as to have this effect.

By combining (33), (34), and (35), we can compute the full effect of monetary shocks on the interest rate:

$$\frac{i_t - i_0}{1 + i_0} = \frac{(\mu + \rho - \theta - \mu\rho\mathcal{L})\varepsilon_t}{\theta(1 - \rho\mathcal{L})(1 - \mu\mathcal{L})} \tag{36}$$

We first see that if $\mu + \rho > 1$, the Ricardian version of the model ($\theta = 1$) always delivers an increase in interest rates on impact in response to monetary injections. We thus obtain the traditional "inflationary expectations effect."

Let us now move to the non-Ricardian case $\theta > 1$. Looking at formula (36), we see that the first period impact $\mu + \rho - \theta$ is negative as soon as

$$\theta > \mu + \rho \tag{37}$$

We will see next that this liquidity effect is persistent, and that condition (37) is actually sufficient for a monetary injection to have a negative effect on the interest rate, not only in the current period, but in all subsequent periods as well. Formula (36) can indeed be rewritten as

$$\frac{i_t - i_0}{1 + i_0} = \frac{1}{\theta(\mu - \rho)} \left[\frac{\rho(\theta - \rho)\varepsilon_t}{1 - \rho\mathcal{L}} - \frac{\mu(\theta - \mu)\varepsilon_t}{1 - \mu\mathcal{L}} \right] \tag{38}$$

Equation (38) can be expressed as a distributed lag of all past innovations in money ε_{t-j}, $j \geq 0$:

$$\frac{i_t - i_0}{1 + i_0} = \sum_{j=0}^{\infty} \varkappa_j \varepsilon_{t-j} \tag{39}$$

with

$$\varkappa_j = \frac{\rho^{j+1}(\theta - \rho) - \mu^{j+1}(\theta - \mu)}{\theta(\mu - \rho)} \tag{40}$$

We want to show now that condition (37) is a sufficient condition for $\varkappa_j < 0$ for all j. This is done simply by rewriting (40) as

$$\varkappa_j = \frac{\mu + \rho - \theta}{\theta} \left(\frac{\mu^{j+1} - \rho^{j+1}}{\mu - \rho} \right) - \frac{\mu\rho}{\theta} \left(\frac{\mu^j - \rho^j}{\mu - \rho} \right) \qquad (41)$$

The second term is always negative or zero. The first term is negative if $\theta > \mu + \rho$. So condition (37) is sufficient for the non-Ricardian liquidity effect to dominate the usual inflationary expectations effect, not only on impact but for all subsequent periods as well.

3.8   Conclusions

We developed in this chapter a new mechanism by which liquidity effects are introduced into dynamic monetary models. The basic channel is the following: (1) in a non-Ricardian economy accumulated financial assets represent, at least partly, real wealth to the generations alive (the Pigou effect) and (2) this Pigou effect gives rise to a liquidity effect as follows: An increase in money raises prices, which decreases the real value of financial wealth. Because of the wealth effect this reduces aggregate demand. In order to maintain aggregate demand at the market-clearing level the real interest rate must go down. This creates, ceteris paribus, the liquidity effect.

3.9   References

This chapter is adapted from Bénassy (2006b).

The liquidity effect dates back to Keynes (1936) and Hicks (1937). Some evidence is provided, for example, by Christiano and Eichenbaum (1992).

One can find in the earlier literature a few DSGE models which produce a liquidity effect with different mechanisms. Two prominent ones are:

• Models of limited participation (Lucas 1990; Christiano and Eichenbaum 1992; Fuerst 1992), where households cannot adapt immediately their financial portfolios when a monetary policy shock occurs.

• Models of sticky prices (Jeanne 1994; Christiano, Eichenbaum, and Evans 1997), where prices are preset in advance. The liquidity effect occurs if the intertemporal elasticity of substitution in consumption is sufficiently low.

Appendix: Proofs of Propositions 3.1 and 3.2

We prove in this appendix propositions 3.1 and 3.2. We actually need to prove only proposition 3.2, which is more general and corresponds to the following distribution of income and taxes over time:

$$y_{jt} = \psi^{t-j} y_t, \quad \tau_{jt} = \psi^{t-j} \tau_t \tag{42}$$

where y_t and τ_t are the income and taxes of a newborn agent in period t. Proposition 3.1 corresponds to the particular case where $\psi = 1$. Let us recall the dynamic equation in proposition 3.2:

$$\psi E_t(P_{t+1} Y_{t+1}) = \beta(1 + n)(1 + i_t) P_t Y_t - (1 - \beta)(1 + n - \psi)\Omega_{t+1} \tag{43}$$

The proof of proposition 3.2 is achieved in a few steps.

The Consumer's Problem

Consider the household's budget equation where, in view of (42), income y_{jt} and taxes τ_{jt} depend on the date j the household was born:

$$\omega_{jt+1} = (1 + i_t)\omega_{jt} + P_t y_{jt} - P_t \tau_{jt} - P_t c_{jt} - i_t m_{jt} \tag{44}$$

We assume that i_t is strictly positive, so the household always satisfies the cash-in-advance constraint exactly. Consequently $m_{jt} = P_t c_{jt}$, and the budget constraint (44) is rewritten as

$$\omega_{jt+1} = (1 + i_t)\omega_{jt} + P_t y_{jt} - P_t \tau_{jt} - (1 + i_t)P_t c_{jt} \tag{45}$$

Maximizing the utility function subject to the sequence of these budget constraints yields the following first-order conditions:

$$\frac{1}{P_t c_{jt}} = \beta(1 + i_t)E_t\left(\frac{1}{P_{t+1} c_{jt+1}}\right) \tag{46}$$

Intertemporal Budget Constraints

As before, we use the following discount factors:

$$D_t = \prod_{s=0}^{t-1} \frac{1}{1+i_s}, \quad D_0 = 1 \tag{47}$$

We take the household's budget equation (45) and apply the discount factors (47) to this budget constraint:

$$D_{s+1}\omega_{js+1} = D_s\omega_{js} + D_{s+1}P_s(y_{js} - \tau_{js}) - D_sP_sc_{js} \tag{48}$$

Then we take the expectation of this equation as of time t:

$$E_t(D_{s+1}\omega_{js+1}) = E_t[D_s\omega_{js} + D_{s+1}P_s(y_{js} - \tau_{js}) - D_sP_sc_{js}] \tag{49}$$

If we aggregate all constraints (49) from time t to infinity, and assume that $D_s\omega_{js}$ goes to zero as s goes to infinity (the transversality condition), we obtain the intertemporal budget constraint of the household, in expected terms:

$$E_t \sum_{s=t}^{\infty} D_sP_sc_{js} = D_t\omega_{jt} + E_t \sum_{s=t}^{\infty} D_{s+1}P_s(y_{js} - \tau_{js}) \tag{50}$$

The Consumption Function

Using the discount factors (47), we rewrite the first-order condition (46) as

$$\frac{1}{D_sP_sc_{js}} = \beta E_s\left(\frac{1}{D_{s+1}P_{s+1}c_{js+1}}\right) \tag{51}$$

We approximate (51) to the first order as

$$E_s(D_{s+1}P_{s+1}c_{js+1}) = \beta D_sP_sc_{js} \tag{52}$$

Taking the expectation as of time t of both sides obtains

$$E_t(D_{s+1}P_{s+1}c_{js+1}) = \beta E_t(D_sP_sc_{js}) \tag{53}$$

We repeatedly apply formula (53) to get

$$E_t(D_s P_s c_{js}) = \beta^{s-t} D_t P_t c_{jt} \tag{54}$$

Thus

$$E_t \sum_{s=t}^{\infty} D_s P_s c_{js} = \frac{D_t P_t c_{jt}}{1 - \beta} \tag{55}$$

Inserting (55) into formula (50), we find the consumption function for agents born in period j:

$$D_t P_t c_{jt} = (1 - \beta) \left[D_t \omega_{jt} + E_t \sum_{s=t}^{\infty} D_{s+1} P_s (y_{js} - \tau_{js}) \right]$$

$$= (1 - \beta) \left[D_t \omega_{jt} + E_t \sum_{s=t}^{\infty} D_{s+1} \psi^{s-j} P_s (y_s - \tau_s) \right] \tag{56}$$

There are $N_j - N_{j-1}$ households in generation j. So, summing over all generations $j \le t$, we obtain total consumption C_t:

$$D_t P_t C_t = (1 - \beta) \left[D_t \Omega_t + E_t \sum_{j=-\infty}^{t} (N_j - N_{j-1}) \sum_{s=t}^{\infty} D_{s+1} \psi^{s-j} P_s (y_s - \tau_s) \right]$$

$$= (1 - \beta) \left[D_t \Omega_t + E_t \sum_{s=t}^{\infty} D_{s+1} \psi^{s-t} P_s (y_s - \tau_s) \right.$$

$$\left. \times \sum_{j=-\infty}^{t} \psi^{t-j} (N_j - N_{j-1}) \right] \tag{57}$$

Now let us define

$$\mathcal{N}_t = \sum_{j=-\infty}^{t} \psi^{t-j} (N_j - N_{j-1}) \tag{58}$$

If $N_t = (1 + n)^t$, $n > 0$, then

$$\mathcal{N}_t = \frac{nN_t}{1 + n - \psi} \tag{59}$$

We have

$$y_t = \frac{Y_t}{\mathcal{N}_t}, \quad \tau_t = \frac{T_t}{\mathcal{N}_t} \tag{60}$$

Aggregate consumption (equation 57) is therefore given by

$$D_t P_t C_t = (1 - \beta) \left[D_t \Omega_t + \mathcal{N}_t E_t \sum_{s=t}^{\infty} D_{s+1} \psi^{s-t} P_s (y_s - \tau_s) \right] \tag{61}$$

Intertemporal Equilibrium

In equilibrium we have $C_t = Y_t$, so equation (61) becomes

$$D_t P_t Y_t = (1 - \beta) \left[D_t \Omega_t + \mathcal{N}_t E_t \sum_{s=t}^{\infty} D_{s+1} \psi^{s-t} P_s (y_s - \tau_s) \right] \tag{62}$$

We divide both sides by $\mathcal{N}_t$ and use $Y_t = \mathcal{N}_t y_t$ to obtain

$$D_t P_t y_t = (1 - \beta) \left[\frac{D_t \Omega_t}{\mathcal{N}_t} + E_t \sum_{s=t}^{\infty} D_{s+1} \psi^{s-t} P_s (y_s - \tau_s) \right] \tag{63}$$

We can rewrite this equation for $t + 1$ and take the expectation as of t:

$$E_t(D_{t+1} P_{t+1} y_{t+1})$$

$$= (1 - \beta) \left[\frac{D_{t+1} \Omega_{t+1}}{\mathcal{N}_{t+1}} + E_t \sum_{s=t+1}^{\infty} D_{s+1} \psi^{s-t-1} P_s (y_s - \tau_s) \right] \tag{64}$$

Next we multiply (64) by ψ and subtract (63) from it:

$$\psi E_t(D_{t+1}P_{t+1}y_{t+1}) - D_tP_ty_t$$

$$= (1 - \beta)\left[\frac{\psi D_{t+1}\Omega_{t+1}}{\mathcal{N}_{t+1}} - \frac{D_t\Omega_t}{\mathcal{N}_t} - D_{t+1}P_t(y_t - \tau_t)\right] \quad (65)$$

We multiply the government's budget equation (11) by $D_{t+1}/\mathcal{N}_t$:

$$\frac{D_t\Omega_t}{\mathcal{N}_t} = \frac{D_{t+1}\Omega_{t+1}}{\mathcal{N}_t} + D_{t+1}P_t\tau_t + (D_t - D_{t+1})P_ty_t \quad (66)$$

After inserting (66) into (65), we have

$$\psi E_t(D_{t+1}P_{t+1}y_{t+1}) = \beta D_tP_ty_t + (1 - \beta)\left(\frac{\psi}{\mathcal{N}_{t+1}} - \frac{1}{\mathcal{N}_t}\right)D_{t+1}\Omega_{t+1} \quad (67)$$

We proceed to multiply (67) by $\mathcal{N}_{t+1}/D_{t+1}$:

$$\psi E_t(P_{t+1}Y_{t+1}) = \beta\frac{\mathcal{N}_{t+1}}{\mathcal{N}_t}(1 + i_t)P_tY_t - (1 - \beta)\left(\frac{\mathcal{N}_{t+1}}{\mathcal{N}_t} - \psi\right)\Omega_{t+1} \quad (68)$$

Taking $\mathcal{N}_{t+1}/\mathcal{N}_t = N_{t+1}/N_t = 1 + n$ from (59), we finally obtain

$$\psi E_t(P_{t+1}Y_{t+1}) = \beta(1 + n)(1 + i_t)P_tY_t - (1 - \beta)(1 + n - \psi)\Omega_{t+1} \quad (69)$$

which is equation (27).

4

Interest Rate Rules and Price Determinacy

4.1 Introduction

We continue our investigation of monetary issues in non-Ricardian economies with a topic that has been largely debated in recent years, that of price determinacy under interest rate rules where the nominal interest rate reacts to various endogenous variables, and particularly to the rate of inflation. Indeed such interest rate rules have come under renewed scrutiny following Taylor's (1993) seminal article. We will be concerned in this chapter with interest rate rules in the framework of dynamic non-Ricardian models. We will notably examine two particularly famous results. The first rule, which originates with the article by Sargent and Wallace (1975), basically says that under a pure nominal interest rate peg, there is nominal indeterminacy (as we saw in chapter 1). The second rule is often referred to as the "Taylor principle."[1] The basic idea is that in order to make prices determinate the central bank should respond "aggressively" to inflation. When interest rates respond only to inflation,

---

1. It should be noted that although Taylor (1993) recommends a strong response of interest rates to inflation, this is more for optimality reasons than to ensure price determinacy as in this chapter. The optimality aspects of the Taylor principle will be studied later in chapter 10.

a classic result is that, in order to have determinate prices, nominal interest rates should respond more than 100 percent to inflation.

As we will see, both results turn out to be true in rigorous models of "Ricardian" economies populated with a single dynasty of consumers. But, as we saw in chapter 1, these economies have, as far as monetary issues are concerned, a number of peculiar properties. So in this and the next chapters we will extend the analysis of interest rate rules to non-Ricardian economies where new agents enter in each period and observe whether or not this makes a difference for the analysis. We will see that it does.

We shall actually see that considering non-Ricardian instead of Ricardian economies dramatically modifies the answers to the two questions above. Notably:

• A pure interest rate peg is fully consistent with local price determinacy provided that the interest rate satisfies a natural "rate-of-return" condition.
• Prices can be determinate even if the nominal interest rate responds less than 100 percent to inflation.

4.2   The Model and Policy

The present model is exactly the same as the model of chapter 2 (section 2.2). We will be, however, more specific about government and policy. The government now includes a fiscal authority (which sets taxes) and a monetary authority (which sets nominal interest rates).

4.2.1   Monetary Policies

Unlike in the previous chapter, where the quantity of money was the instrument of monetary policy, we consider here interest rate rules where the nominal interest rate is the central instrument of monetary policy.

As indicated in the introduction, we will study two types of monetary policies. The first is interest rate pegging, which consists in setting the nominal interest rate i_t exogenously. In most of what follows we take, for simplicity of exposition, the particular case where the interest rate is pegged at a constant value:

$$i_t = i_0 \qquad \forall t \tag{1}$$

The second type of policy we will consider consists of Taylor rules (Taylor 1993), through which the nominal interest rate responds to inflation. If we denote the inflation rate as

$$\pi_t = \log \Pi_t = \log\left(\frac{P_t}{P_{t-1}}\right) \tag{2}$$

then a typical Taylor rule is written in a loglinear way[2] as

$$i_t - i_0 = \phi(\pi_t - \pi_0), \qquad \phi \geq 0 \tag{3}$$

where π_0 is the long-run rate of inflation and i_0 a target interest rate. The "Taylor principle" suggests that, for prices to be determinate, the coefficient ϕ should be greater than 1.

4.2.2 Fiscal Policy

Since our focus is not on fiscal policy, in order to simplify the dynamics below, in a first step, we assume that the tax policy of the government consists in balancing the budget period by period.[3] Taxes will thus cover exactly interest payments on bonds:

$$P_t T_t = i_t B_t \tag{4}$$

4.3   The Dynamic Equilibrium

We saw in chapter 2 (proposition 2.1) that the following dynamic equation holds:

$$P_{t+1} Y_{t+1} = \beta(1 + n)(1 + i_t)P_t Y_t - (1 - \beta)n\Omega_{t+1} \tag{5}$$

Now let us recall from the previous chapter the government budget constraint:

$$\Omega_{t+1} = (1 + i_t)\Omega_t - i_t M_t - P_t T_t \tag{6}$$

---

2. We can use a loglinear approximation because in this chapter we will study local determinacy only. Global determinacy is studied in the next chapter.

3. A more general policy is considered in section 4.9.

Combining (4), (6), and $\Omega_t = M_t + B_t$ we immediately see that under the balanced budget policy (4) total financial wealth will remain constant:

$$\Omega_t = \Omega_0 \qquad \forall t \tag{7}$$

The dynamic equation (5) then becomes

$$P_{t+1} Y_{t+1} = \beta(1 + n)(1 + i_t)P_t Y_t - (1 - \beta)n\Omega_0 \tag{8}$$

4.4   Ricardian Economies and the Taylor Principle

Here we briefly review some traditional results on price determinacy under interest rate rules in the Ricardian setting. In the Ricardian model $n = 0$, and equation (5) becomes

$$P_{t+1} Y_{t+1} = \beta(1 + i_t)P_t Y_t \tag{9}$$

which is the traditional aggregate dynamic equation. Using this equation and the intertemporal budget constraint we already saw in chapter 1 that exogenously pegging the nominal interest rate i_t leads to nominal indeterminacy, as was pointed out by Sargent and Wallace (1975).

4.4.1   The Taylor Principle

Let us now consider more general interest rate rules that take the form (equation 3)

$$i_t - i_0 = \phi(\pi_t - \pi_0) \qquad \phi \geq 0 \tag{10}$$

We can loglinearize equation (9), using $Y_{t+1}/Y_t = \zeta$, to obtain

$$\pi_{t+1} = i_t + \log\left(\frac{\beta}{\zeta}\right) - n \tag{11}$$

Then we insert (10) into (11), which gives

$$\pi_{t+1} = \phi(\pi_t - \pi_0) + i_0 + \log\left(\frac{\beta}{\zeta}\right) - n \tag{12}$$

This can be rewritten as

$$\pi_t = \frac{\pi_{t+1}}{\phi} + \frac{\phi\pi_0 - i_0 - \log(\beta/\zeta) + n}{\phi} \tag{13}$$

Clearly the inflation rate will be determinate if $\phi > 1$ (the Taylor principle). Since the past price is predetermined, a determinate inflation rate also means a determinate price. So the Taylor principle holds in this Ricardian framework, at least for local determinacy.

4.5 Determinacy under an Interest Rate Peg

We now revert to the more general non-Ricardian framework, and consider the first problem we mentioned, that of a pure interest rate peg. We shall first study the Walrasian version of the model. To simplify the exposition we consider here the particular case where the pegged interest rate is constant over time:

$$i_t = i_0 \qquad \forall t \tag{14}$$

The case of a variable pegged interest rate is treated in the appendix at the end of the chapter. Given (14), the dynamic equation (8) is rewritten as

$$P_{t+1} Y_{t+1} = \beta(1 + n)(1 + i_0)P_t Y_t - (1 - \beta)n\Omega_0 \tag{15}$$

In what follows it will be convenient to use nominal income $\mathcal{Y}_t$ as our working variable:

$$\mathcal{Y}_t = P_t Y_t \tag{16}$$

so that (15) is rewritten as

$$\mathcal{Y}_{t+1} = \beta(1 + n)(1 + i_0)\mathcal{Y}_t - (1 - \beta)n\Omega_0 \tag{17}$$

We see that there is a locally determinate solution in $\mathcal{Y}_t$ provided that

$$\theta = \beta(1 + n)(1 + i_0) > 1 \tag{18}$$

This solution is given by

$$y_t = y_0 = \frac{(1-\beta)n\Omega_0}{\beta(1+n)(1+i_0)-1} \tag{19}$$

4.6 Taylor Rules

We continue with the non-Ricardian model and turn to the more general Taylor rules (3). To see whether the Taylor principle still holds, we loglinearize equation (8) and obtain the following equation:

$$p_{t+1} + y_{t+1} = \theta(p_t + y_t) + \varrho(i_t - i_0) \tag{20}$$

with

$$\theta = \beta(1+n)(1+i_0), \quad \varrho = \beta(1+n) \tag{21}$$

Then we combine (20) with the interest rate equation (10), and we obtain, omitting irrelevant constant terms,

$$p_{t+1} = \theta p_t + \varrho\phi\pi_t \tag{22}$$

This can actually be rewritten as a two-dimensional dynamic system in inflation and the price level

$$p_t = \pi_t + p_{t-1} \tag{23}$$

$$\pi_{t+1} = (\theta-1)p_t + \phi\varrho\pi_t = (\theta-1+\varrho\phi)\pi_t + (\theta-1)p_{t-1} \tag{24}$$

or in matrix form, lagging variables one period,

$$\begin{bmatrix} \pi_t \\ p_{t-1} \end{bmatrix} = \begin{bmatrix} \theta-1+\varrho\phi & \theta-1 \\ 1 & 1 \end{bmatrix} \begin{bmatrix} \pi_{t-1} \\ p_{t-2} \end{bmatrix} \tag{25}$$

The characteristic polynomial is

$$\Psi(\lambda) = \phi\varrho(1-\lambda) + \lambda(\lambda-\theta) = \lambda^2 - (\theta+\phi\varrho)\lambda + \phi\varrho \tag{26}$$

We have one predetermined variable (the past price) and a nonpredetermined one (inflation). By the Blanchard-Kahn (1980) conditions, there will be a determinate solution if the polynomial $\Psi(\lambda)$ has one root of modulus smaller than 1, and the other greater than 1. So we compute

$$\Psi(0) = \varrho\phi \geq 0 \qquad (27)$$

$$\Psi(1) = 1 - \theta \qquad (28)$$

Because $\Psi(\lambda)$ goes to infinity when λ goes to infinity, we see that if $\theta > 1$, one root is between zero and one and the other is greater than one. Again, $\theta > 1$ is a sufficient condition for local determinacy, and whether ϕ is above or below 1 is not important anymore.

4.7 Economic Interpretations

We just found that prices are determined if $n > 0$ and condition (18), meaning $\theta > 1$, is satisfied. This holds both for an interest rate peg and for a Taylor rule like (3). This is a very substantial change, and it is time to give some economic interpretations.

4.7.1 The Pigou, or Real Balance Effect

When one looks at the dynamic equations (5) and (8), it appears clearly that a feature that drives most of the results is the presence of financial assets Ω_t in the dynamic equations. This is indeed a sort of "nominal anchor," which is instrumental in tying down the value of prices. We already noted that this presence of financial assets in various behavioral equations has a history in the literature under the names of Pigou effect (Pigou 1943) or real balance effect (Patinkin 1956), and its importance is apparent here once again.

4.7.2 Determinacy and the Return on Financial Assets

So if $n > 0$, we have a Pigou effect. But this not the end of the story. Clearly this effect is really operative only if the agents actually desire to hold money and financial assets. And this is where the central condition (18) sets in. In order to better interpret it, let us rewrite (18) in the following form:

$$\zeta(1 + n)(1 + i_0) > \frac{\zeta}{\beta} \qquad (29)$$

Note that the left-hand side is the real rate of return on bonds. Indeed because $P_t Y_t = \mathcal{Y}_t$ is constant, and real resources grow at the rate $\zeta(1 + n)$, in the steady state prices decrease at the rate $\zeta(1 + n)$, and therefore the real rate of interest is $\zeta(1 + n)(1 + i_0)$.

Now ζ/β on the right-hand side of (29) is the "autarkic" gross real interest rate ξ, meaning the real rate of return that would prevail if agents of each generation traded only between themselves, in total autarky from the other generations (see chapter 2, section 2.7).

Therefore conditions (18) or (29) essentially say that the real rate of return of bonds must be superior to the autarkic rate of return. We see that this condition is very much similar to that found by Wallace (1980) for the viability of money in the traditional Samuelsonian (1958) overlapping generations model. But there is a difference. In Wallace (1980) the only financial store of value is money, so the rate of return condition concerns the return on money. In our case this condition concerns the return on bonds, and accordingly the nominal interest rate plays a major role.

We will call this condition the financial dominance (FD) criterion. A more general version will be given in the next chapter when we study global determinacy.

4.8   The Taylor Principle with a Phillips Curve

So far we have studied the issue of price determinacy under the assumption of full market clearing. But the issue of price determinacy under interest rate rules has been very often studied in models with nonclearing markets where output is demand determined and prices adjust partially according to a forward-looking Phillips curve of the type

$$\pi_t = \frac{1}{f} E_t \pi_{t+1} + g y_t, \qquad f > 1, g > 0 \qquad (30)$$

Our objective in this section is to show that the results we obtained above in a Walrasian economy extend to this framework as well. In our setting a rigorous derivation of such a Phillips curve would take us a bit too far, notably with an infinity of households, all with different marginal utilities of income. So we will simply take the Phillips curve (30) as given, and show that going from a Ricardian to a non-Ricardian framework leads again to major changes.

As before, the monetary authority uses an interest rate rule of the Taylor type:

$$i_t - i_0 = \phi(\pi_t - \pi_0) \tag{31}$$

In order to better highlight the differences, let us now begin with the Ricardian version of the model.

4.8.1 The Ricardian Case

Output is now endogenous, and assumed to be demand determined, so equation (8) is still valid. Loglinearizing it, we obtain

$$y_{t+1} = y_t + \log \beta + (i_t - \pi_{t+1}) \tag{32}$$

Combining (32) with the interest rule (31) yields

$$y_{t+1} = y_t + \log \beta + i_0 + \phi(\pi_t - \pi_0) - \pi_{t+1} \tag{33}$$

We can rewrite (30) and (33) by replacing $E_t \pi_{t+1}$ by π_{t+1}, since the model is deterministic, and omitting constants:

$$\pi_{t+1} = f(\pi_t - gy_t) \tag{34}$$

$$y_{t+1} = (1 + fg)y_t + (\phi - f)\pi_t \tag{35}$$

This can be rewritten in matrix form as

$$\begin{bmatrix} y_t \\ \pi_t \end{bmatrix} = \begin{bmatrix} 1 + fg & \phi - f \\ -fg & f \end{bmatrix} \begin{bmatrix} y_{t-1} \\ \pi_{t-1} \end{bmatrix} \tag{36}$$

The characteristic polynomial is

$$\Psi(\lambda) = \lambda^2 - (1 + f + fg)\lambda + f(1 + g\phi) \tag{37}$$

$$\Psi(0) = f(1 + g\phi) > 0 \tag{38}$$

$$\Psi(1) = fg(\phi - 1) \tag{39}$$

If $\phi < 1$, we have one root between 0 and 1. Since neither y_t and π_t are predetermined, this means that we have indeterminacy. On the other hand, if $\phi > 1$, the two roots have modulus greater than 1, and we have determinacy. We thus find again that the Taylor principle holds in this Ricardian framework.

4.8.2   The Non-Ricardian Case

Let us now move to the non-Ricardian economy. Equation (8) still holds. Loglinearizing it, we find that output, inflation, and prices are linked by the following equation:

$$y_{t+1} + p_{t+1} = \theta(y_t + p_t) + \varrho(i_t - i_0) \tag{40}$$

where the values of θ and ϱ are given in equation (21). We can express y_{t+1}, π_{t+1}, and p_t as a function of the corresponding lagged variables,

$$p_t = \pi_t + p_{t-1} \tag{41}$$

$$\pi_{t+1} = f(\pi_t - gy_t) \tag{42}$$

$$y_{t+1} = (\theta + fg)y_t + (\theta - 1 + \phi\varrho - f)\pi_t + (\theta - 1)p_{t-1} \tag{43}$$

or in matrix form (omitting the constants),

$$\begin{bmatrix} y_t \\ \pi_t \\ p_{t-1} \end{bmatrix} = \begin{bmatrix} \theta + fg & \theta - 1 + \phi\varrho - f & \theta - 1 \\ -fg & f & 0 \\ 0 & 1 & 1 \end{bmatrix} \begin{bmatrix} y_{t-1} \\ \pi_{t-1} \\ p_{t-2} \end{bmatrix} \tag{44}$$

The characteristic polynomial is

$$\Psi(\lambda) = (1 - \lambda)(f - \lambda)(\theta - \lambda) + fg\varrho\phi(1 - \lambda) + fg\lambda(\lambda - \theta) \tag{45}$$

We now show that $\theta > 1$ is again a sufficient condition for determinacy. There is one predetermined variable (the past price) and two nonpredetermined variables (output and inflation). So there will be a determinate solution if the polynomial $\Psi(\lambda)$ has one root of modulus smaller than 1, and two roots of modulus greater than 1. Let us compute

$$\Psi(0) = f(\theta + g\varrho\phi) > 0 \tag{46}$$

$$\Psi(1) = fg(1 - \theta) \tag{47}$$

Let us assume $\theta > 1$ so that one root is between zero and one. Since the product of the three roots is $\Psi(0) = f(\theta + g\varrho\phi) > 1$, the only possible case where the two remaining roots are not of modulus greater than 1 is that where we have two negative roots, one smaller than -1 and one greater. In that case we would have $\Psi(-1) < 0$. Therefore, together with $\theta > 1$, $\Psi(-1) > 0$ is a sufficient condition for determinacy. So we compute

$$\Psi(-1) = 2(1 + f)(1 + \theta) + 2fg\varrho\phi + fg(1 + \theta) > 0 \tag{48}$$

To summarize, if $\theta > 1$, we have one root between zero and one, and two roots of modulus greater than one. The inflation rate is then determinate and thus so is the price level.

4.9 Generalizations

We study here two generalizations of the model we have used so far. First, the hypothesis of budget balance is replaced by the possibility of constant growth of government liabilities. Second, we introduce decreasing resources over time, as in chapter 2, section 2.6. This last generalization will allow us notably to explain why there was no problem of determinacy in the OLG model of chapter 1.

4.9.1 Variable Government Liabilities

We start with a generalization of the fiscal policy (4), and assume that instead of balancing the budget, the government engineers through taxes proportional expansions (or reductions) of its financial liabilities Ω_t (such an experiment was studied in Wallace 1980). We want to see how this affects the conditions for determinacy. More precisely, let us assume that taxes take the form

$$P_t T_t = i_t B_t + (1 - \gamma)\Omega_t, \qquad \gamma > 0 \tag{49}$$

Then the evolution of Ω_t is given by a combination of (6), (49), and

$\Omega_t = M_t + B_t$:

$$\Omega_{t+1} = \gamma \Omega_t \tag{50}$$

Most of the analysis seen previously is still valid, and in particular equation (5) which we recall here:

$$P_{t+1} Y_{t+1} = \beta(1+n)(1+i_t)P_t Y_t - (1-\beta)n\Omega_{t+1} \tag{51}$$

The dynamic system consists of equations (50) and (51). Dividing (51) by (50), we obtain

$$\frac{P_{t+1} Y_{t+1}}{\Omega_{t+1}} = \frac{\beta(1+n)(1+i_t)}{\gamma} \frac{P_t Y_t}{\Omega_t} - (1-\beta)n \tag{52}$$

We first study the determinacy conditions for a pure interest rate peg $i_t = i_0$. Inserting this into (52), we see that the condition for determinacy is

$$\beta(1+n)(1+i_0) > \gamma \tag{53}$$

or $\theta > \gamma$. This equation has in fact an interpretation very similar to that of equation (18). Indeed it can be rewritten as

$$\frac{\zeta(1+n)(1+i_0)}{\gamma} > \frac{\zeta}{\beta} \tag{54}$$

Since nominal assets are growing at the rate γ, the long-run rate of inflation is $\gamma/\zeta(1+n)$. The left-hand side is then the real rate of return on financial assets, and the rest of the intuition given in section 4.7 continues to hold.

Next we shall see that the "expanded" condition (53) is actually sufficient for determinacy in all the non-Ricardian cases we considered in sections 4.6 and 4.8. We begin by loglinearizing equation (52):

$$p_{t+1} + y_{t+1} - \omega_{t+1} = \frac{\theta}{\gamma}(p_t + y_t - \omega_t) + \frac{\varrho\phi}{\gamma}(\pi_t - \pi_0) \tag{55}$$

where θ and ϱ are the same as in (21). We see that all of our analysis in the previous sections is valid provided that we replace p_t by $p_t - \omega_t$ and the parameters θ and ϱ by θ/γ and ϱ/γ respectively.

We should note that condition (53) shows most clearly the trade-offs faced by the government on fiscal and monetary policy. Indeed a stricter fiscal policy (low γ) allows government to conduct a less rigorous monetary policy (low i_0), and conversely, a stricter monetary policy (high i_0) allows government to conduct a less rigorous fiscal policy (high γ).

4.9.2 Decreasing Resources

We shall now consider a second generalization, and assume that relative endowments and taxes decrease in time at the rate $\psi \le 1$ as follows:

$$y_{jt} = \psi^{t-j} y_t, \quad \tau_{jt} = \psi^{t-j} \tau_t, \quad j \le t \qquad (56)$$

where y_t and τ_t are the income and taxes of a newborn agent in period t. We saw in chapter 2 (proposition 2.2) that under this more general hypothesis the dynamic equation (5) is replaced by

$$\psi P_{t+1} Y_{t+1} = \beta(1+n)(1+i_t)P_t Y_t - (1-\beta)(1+n-\psi)\Omega_{t+1} \qquad (57)$$

Again we take the case of a nominal interest rate peg $i_t = i_0$ with the balanced budget fiscal policy (4). We rewrite (57) as

$$\psi P_{t+1} Y_{t+1} = \beta(1+n)(1+i_0)P_t Y_t - (1-\beta)(1+n-\psi)\Omega_0 \qquad (58)$$

The condition for determinacy becomes

$$\frac{\beta(1+n)(1+i_0)}{\psi} > 1 \qquad (59)$$

We see that with a low value of ψ this determinacy condition becomes easier to satisfy.

In chapter 1 we studied an overlapping generations model in which, unlike in the Ricardian model, price determinacy is always ensured. We shall now see that we can mimic this result in the model of this section. Households in the OLG model of chapter 1 have no resources in the second period of their lives. This would correspond here to the value $\psi = 0$. We insert this value into (58) and immediately find that

$$P_t Y_t = \frac{(1 - \beta)\Omega_0}{\beta(1 + i_0)} \qquad (60)$$

We see that we also have full price determinacy.

4.10   Conclusions

We have seen that going from a Ricardian to a non-Ricardian framework changes dramatically the conditions for local price determinacy under interest rate rules. It is usually found in a Ricardian framework that interest rate pegging leads to nominal indeterminacy, and that a more than one to one response of interest rates to inflation (the Taylor principle) leads to price determinacy.

We found instead that a strong response of the interest rate rule to inflation is not necessary for price determinacy, which can be achieved even under an interest rate peg. We identified sufficient conditions for determinacy (conditions 18 or 53), which express that the real rate of return on nominal assets must be superior to the "autarkic" real rate of return that would prevail if each generation had no trade with other generations. This condition ensures that agents are actually willing to hold money and financial assets in the long run, obviously a critical condition if one wants money to have value and prices to be determinate.

Now all the determinacy conditions we derived in this chapter are local determinacy conditions. In the next chapter we will pose the more demanding question of global determinacy.

4.11   References

This chapter is adapted from Bénassy (2005). Early contributions on the problem of price determinacy under an interest peg in non-Ricardian economies are found in Bénassy (2000) and Cushing (1999).

Early rigorous results on price determinacy in a Ricardian model are found in Leeper (1991). The Taylor principle was initiated in Taylor (1993, 1998). Surveys of interest rate rules can be found, for example, in McCallum (1999), Taylor (1999).

The financial dominance criterion appears in Wallace (1980) in an OLG model with money as a single store of value and Bénassy (2005) in a model with both money and interest-bearing assets.

A few contributions have sought to modify the "traditional" results on interest pegging or the Taylor principle. For example, Benhabib, Schmitt-Grohé, and Uribe (2001b) show the importance of how money enters the utility and production functions. McCallum (1981) advocates linking directly interest rates to a "nominal anchor-like" price level. Roisland (2003) shows that capital income taxation modifies the Taylor principle.

The Phillips curve initiates in Phillips (1958). Forward-looking Phillips curves such as (30) are most often derived from a framework of contracts à la Calvo (1983). They can be also derived from a model with convex costs of changing prices (Rotemberg 1982a, b). See Rotemberg (1987) for an early derivation under both interpretations.

Appendix: Interest Rate Pegging with Variable Interest Rates

We explore here the case where the pegged interest rate can vary in time. Equation (17) is replaced by

$$y_{t+1} = \beta(1 + n)(1 + i_t)y_t - (1 - \beta)n\Omega_0 \tag{61}$$

This equation can be rewritten as

$$y_t = \frac{y_{t+1} + (1 - \beta)n\Omega_0}{\beta(1 + n)(1 + i_t)} \tag{62}$$

A sufficient condition for determinacy is

$$\beta(1 + n)(1 + i_t) > 1 \qquad \forall t \tag{63}$$

We can again use the discount factors:

$$D_t = \prod_{s=0}^{t-1} \frac{1}{1 + i_s} \tag{64}$$

Using the discount factors (64), we can rewrite equation (62) as

$$y_t = \frac{D_{t+1}}{D_t} \frac{y_{t+1} + (1 - \beta)n\Omega_0}{\beta(1 + n)} \tag{65}$$

If condition (63) is satisfied, (65) can be integrated forward as follows:

$$y_t = \frac{(1-\beta)n\Omega}{D_t} \sum_{i=1}^{\infty} \frac{D_{t+i}}{\beta^i(1+n)^i} \qquad (66)$$

5

Global Determinacy

5.1 Introduction

We saw in the previous chapter that moving from a Ricardian to a non-Ricardian framework brought major changes to the conditions of price determinacy in response to interest rate rules. In particular, we saw that although the Taylor principle is rightly considered a condition for price determinacy (at least a local one) in Ricardian economies, in non-Ricardian economies another criterion, the financial dominance criterion, emerged as a relevant alternative.

Now the analysis of the previous chapter was about local determinacy. We study in this chapter the same issue from the point of view of global determinacy. We will find again that in a non-Ricardian framework the Taylor principle is no longer the central determinacy condition. On the other hand, the financial dominance (FD) criterion, which was introduced in the previous chapter, appears to be essential not only for local determinacy but for global determinacy as well.

5.2 The Model

We will use the same model as in the previous chapter (first described in chapter 2, section 2.2). In particular, this model is characterized by the two following dynamic equations:

$$\Omega_{t+1} = (1 + i_t)\Omega_t - i_t M_t - P_t T_t \tag{1}$$

$$P_{t+1} Y_{t+1} = \beta(1 + n)(1 + i_t)P_t Y_t - (1 - \beta)n\Omega_{t+1} \tag{2}$$

We proceed now to examine more precisely the two governmental policies, monetary and fiscal policies.

5.2.1   Monetary Policy

In the preceding chapter we studied local determinacy, and accordingly used a loglinearized version of the interest rate rule. Here we will assume that monetary policy takes the form of "Taylor rules," which links the value of the nominal interest rate to inflation but this time in the more general form:[1]

$$1 + i_t = \Phi(\Pi_t) \tag{3}$$

with

$$\Pi_t = \frac{P_t}{P_{t-1}} \tag{4}$$

This interest rate rule must respect the zero lower bound on the nominal interest rate:

$$\Phi(\Pi_t) \geq 1 \qquad \forall \Pi_t \tag{5}$$

We further assume

$$\Phi'(\Pi_t) \geq 0 \tag{6}$$

An important parameter is the elasticity ϕ of the function Φ:

$$\phi(\Pi_t) = \frac{\Pi_t \Phi(\Pi_t)}{\Phi(\Pi_t)} \tag{7}$$

1. The function Φ gives $1 + i_t$, not i_t, as a function of Π_t because this is the term that appears in the intertemporal maximization conditions.

As we already indicated, the Taylor principle says that this elasticity should be greater than 1. Note that because of the constraint that the nominal interest rate must be greater than zero, the Taylor principle cannot be verified for all values of Π_t. In particular, $\phi(0) = 0$.

5.2.2 Fiscal Policy

Since the object of our study is principally monetary policy, we want to take the simplest possible fiscal policies. If the budget was balanced, taxes would be equal to interest payments on bonds $i_t B_t$. So we would have

$$P_t T_t = i_t B_t \tag{8}$$

Because the rate of expansion of government liabilities will play a substantial role below, we must consider, as in the previous chapter, a more general class of policies, of the form

$$P_t T_t = i_t B_t + (1 - \gamma)\Omega_t, \qquad \gamma > 0 \tag{9}$$

As compared to the balanced budget policy (8), the term $(1 - \gamma)\Omega_t$ has been added. It says that the government may want to withdraw a fraction $1 - \gamma$ of its outstanding financial liabilities. If γ is greater than 1, this actually corresponds to an expansion of government liabilities.

5.2.3 Dynamics

Putting together equations (1), (9), and the definition $\Omega_t = M_t + B_t$, we first find the equation of evolution of Ω_t:

$$\Omega_{t+1} = \gamma\Omega_t \tag{10}$$

Then, combining (2) and (3), we obtain

$$P_{t+1} Y_{t+1} = \beta(1 + n)\Phi(\Pi_t)P_t Y_t - (1 - \beta)n\Omega_{t+1} \tag{11}$$

Equations (10) and (11) are the basic dynamic equations of our model.

5.3 Ricardian Economies and the Taylor Principle

We begin our investigation with the traditional Ricardian version of the model. For that it is enough to take $n = 0$. Equation (11) then simplifies to

$$P_{t+1} Y_{t+1} = \beta \Phi(\Pi_t) P_t Y_t \qquad (12)$$

which, since $Y_{t+1}/Y_t = \zeta$, is rewritten as

$$\Pi_{t+1} = \frac{\beta}{\zeta} \Phi(\Pi_t) = \frac{\Phi(\Pi_t)}{\xi} \qquad (13)$$

where ξ is the autarkic real interest rate that was defined in chapter 2, section 2.7. From (13) the potential steady state values of Π_t, denoted as Π, are solutions of the equation:

$$\frac{\Phi(\Pi)}{\Pi} = \xi \qquad (14)$$

We denote as Π^k, $k = 1, \ldots, K$, the solutions to equation (14), ranked in ascending order. Depending on the shape of the function Φ and the value of ξ, equation (14) can have potentially any number of solutions (including zero).[2] Figure 5.1 represents the case of two solutions, Π^1 and Π^2. We should note that the Taylor principle is verified at Π^2 but not at Π^1.

5.3.1 Local Determinacy

We can linearize equation (13) around a particular potential steady state Π:

$$\Pi_{t+1} - \Pi = \frac{\Phi'(\Pi)}{\xi} (\Pi_t - \Pi) \qquad (15)$$

The condition for local determinacy is thus

---

2. Note that the condition $\phi'(\Pi_t) \geq 0$ is actually sufficient for no more than two solutions.

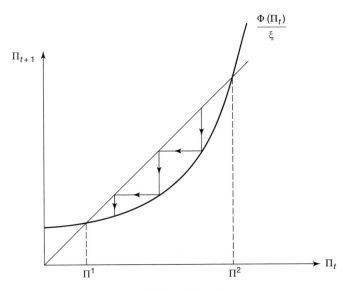

Figure 5.1

$$\Phi'(\Pi) > \xi \tag{16}$$

Combined with (14) this yields

$$\frac{\Pi\Phi'(\Pi)}{\Phi(\Pi t)} = \phi(\Pi) > 1 \tag{17}$$

So, if the elasticity of the function Φ is greater than 1, the inflation rate and the price level are locally determinate. This is the Taylor principle. Nevertheless, we must go further and inquire under which conditions global determinacy holds.

5.3.2 Global Determinacy

Consider the case represented in figure 5.1, with two potential equilibria. As shown, if there is an equilibrium where $\phi(\Pi^2) > 1$, because of the zero lower bound on the nominal interest rate there must be another equilibrium Π^1 where the Taylor principle is not satisfied, meaning where $\phi(\Pi^1) < 1$, and that equilibrium is locally indeterminate. The corresponding dynamics is depicted in figure 5.1, which represents equation (13). Dynamic paths initiating between the two equilibria Π^1 and Π^2 converge toward the indeterminate equilibrium Π^1.

To ensure global determinacy, we must find additional conditions that ensure that such paths are actually not feasible. Continuing with the example of figure 5.1, it is shown in appendix A (proposition 5.3) that a sufficient condition for global determinacy of Π^2 in that case is that besides the Taylor principle $\phi(\Pi^2) > 1$,

$$\Pi^1 < \Pi^* < \Pi^2 \tag{18}$$

where

$$\Pi^* = \frac{\gamma}{\zeta} \tag{19}$$

More generally (proposition 5.3, appendix A at the end of the chapter), if there are K solutions $\Pi^1, \ldots, \Pi^k, \ldots, \Pi^K$ to the equation $\Phi(\Pi) = \xi\Pi$, then Π^K is globally determinate if

$$\phi(\Pi^K) > 1 \tag{20}$$

$$\Pi^{K-1} < \Pi^* < \Pi^K \tag{21}$$

Note that condition (21) is also a sufficient condition for the equilibrium Π^K to satisfy the transversality conditions (appendix C).

So we see that the Taylor principle (20) is still part of the determinacy conditions. It is supplemented, however, by condition (21), which ensures that only the equilibrium corresponding to the highest inflation Π^K is acceptable. We will next see that these determinacy conditions are substantially modified when one moves to a non-Ricardian situation.

5.4   Non-Ricardian Economies: Dynamics and Steady States

We now move to non-Ricardian economies, assuming that $n > 0$.

5.4.1   The Dynamic System

Let us recall the dynamic system (10), (11):

$$\Omega_{t+1} = \gamma\Omega_t \tag{22}$$

$$P_{t+1}Y_{t+1} = \beta(1+n)\Phi(\Pi_t)P_tY_t - (1-\beta)n\Omega_{t+1} \qquad (23)$$

It will actually be convenient in what follows to use as working variables inflation Π_t and the predetermined variable X_t defined as[3]

$$X_t = \frac{\Omega_t}{P_{t-1}Y_{t-1}} \qquad (24)$$

Then the dynamic system (22), (23) is rewritten as

$$X_{t+1} = \Pi^* \frac{X_t}{\Pi_t} \qquad (25)$$

$$\Pi_{t+1} = \frac{\Phi(\Pi_t)}{\zeta} - v\Pi^* \frac{X_t}{\Pi_t} \qquad (26)$$

with

$$\Pi^* = \frac{\gamma}{\zeta(1+n)}, \quad v = \frac{(1-\beta)n}{(1+n)\zeta} \qquad (27)$$

5.4.2 The Two Types of Steady States

From (25) and (26) potential steady states Π and X are solutions of the set of equations:

$$X = \Pi^* \frac{X}{\Pi} \qquad (28)$$

$$\Pi = \frac{\Phi(\Pi)}{\zeta} - vX \qquad (29)$$

We see that there are two types of steady states. We will call them respectively "Ricardian" and "non-Ricardian":

Definition 5.1 *Ricardian equilibria, or equilibria of type $\mathcal{R}$, are the solutions to the system* (28) *and* (29) *characterized by*

---

3. This representation is borrowed from Guillard (2004).

$$X^k = 0, \quad \frac{\Phi(\Pi^k)}{\Pi^k} = \xi, \qquad k = 1, \ldots, K \tag{30}$$

A non-Ricardian equilibrium, or equilibrium of type $\mathcal{N}\mathcal{R}$, is the solution to the system (28) *and* (29) *characterized by*

$$\Pi = \Pi^* = \frac{\gamma}{\zeta(1+n)}, \quad X = X^* = \frac{1}{\nu}\left[\frac{\Phi(\Pi^*)}{\xi} - \Pi^*\right] \tag{31}$$

Steady states of type $\mathcal{R}$ ("Ricardian") are similar to the steady states in Ricardian economies (14), with a supplementary condition for the stationary value of X, which here is equal to zero. In both cases the potential equilibrium rates of inflation are given by equations (14) or (30). The real gross rate of interest R_t is equal to $\xi = \zeta/\beta$, the autarkic rate, whatever the value of the inflation rate.

The (unique) steady state of type $\mathcal{N}\mathcal{R}$ ("non-Ricardian") is more specific to the non-Ricardian environment. The inflation rate Π^* is no longer characterized by the properties of the Taylor rule, but is equal to the rate of growth of government liabilities, γ divided by the rate of growth of output $\zeta(1+n)$, a most traditional formula. The real (gross) rate of interest, denoted R^*, is no longer equal to ξ. For example we can deduce it from the inflation rate by

$$R^* = \frac{\Phi(\Pi^*)}{\Pi^*} \tag{32}$$

5.5   The Financial Dominance Criterion

We saw in the previous chapter that the Taylor principle was replaced, as far as local determinacy is concerned, by a new criterion, which we called the "financial dominance" criterion. This criterion was expressed in a "local" way. Because we will need a more global approach, and this criterion will play an important role in this and the next chapter, we now give a more general definition.

Definition 5.2   *The "financial dominance" (FD) criterion is satisfied for the value of inflation Π if*

$$\frac{\Phi(\Pi)}{\Pi} > \xi \tag{33}$$

In words, the gross real interest rate $\Phi(\Pi)/\Pi$ generated by the interest rate rule is above the autarkic rate ξ. In order to characterize financial dominance with a simple compact parameter, we define

$$\kappa(\Pi) = \frac{1}{\xi} \frac{\Phi(\Pi)}{\Pi} \tag{34}$$

The financial dominance (FD) criterion holds if

$$\kappa(\Pi) > 1 \tag{35}$$

We will see next now this criterion plays a central role for both local and global determinacy.

5.6   Local Determinacy and Financial Dominance

In order to show the respective relevance of the financial dominance and the Taylor principle criteria, we now first study the local determinacy of our potential equilibria. We begin by linearizing the system (25), (26) around a steady state (X, Π). Using (28) and (34), we find

$$\begin{bmatrix} \Pi_{t+1} - \Pi \\ X_{t+1} - X \end{bmatrix} = \begin{bmatrix} \phi\kappa + \dfrac{vX}{\Pi} & -\dfrac{v\Pi^*}{\Pi} \\ -\dfrac{X}{\Pi} & \dfrac{\Pi^*}{\Pi} \end{bmatrix} \begin{bmatrix} \Pi_t - \Pi \\ X_t - X \end{bmatrix} \tag{36}$$

with

$$\phi = \phi(\Pi), \quad \kappa = \kappa(\Pi), \quad \Pi^* = \frac{\gamma}{(1+n)\zeta} \tag{37}$$

The characteristic polynomial corresponding to this linearized dynamic system is given by

$$\Psi(\lambda) = (\lambda - \phi\kappa)\left(\lambda - \frac{\Pi^*}{\Pi}\right) - \frac{\lambda vX}{\Pi} \tag{38}$$

Then, using (29) and (34), we rewrite (38) as

$$\Psi(\lambda) = (\lambda - \phi\kappa)\left(\lambda - \frac{\Pi^*}{\Pi}\right) + (1 - \kappa)\frac{\Pi^*}{\Pi} \qquad (39)$$

The determinacy conditions will differ depending on whether the equilibrium is of type $\mathcal{R}$ or $\mathcal{NR}$, as defined in section 5.4, so we study them in turn.

5.6.1 Equilibria of Type $\mathcal{R}$

Consider a steady state Π^k of type $\mathcal{R}$ (definition 5.1). In this case we have $\kappa = 1$, so the corresponding characteristic polynomial is

$$\Psi_{\mathcal{R}}(\lambda) = (\lambda - \phi^k)\left(\lambda - \frac{\Pi^*}{\Pi^k}\right) \qquad (40)$$

This characteristic polynomial has two roots:

$$\lambda_1 = \phi^k, \quad \lambda_2 = \frac{\Pi^*}{\Pi^k} \qquad (41)$$

There is local determinacy if one of these roots is of modulus greater than 1, the other smaller than 1, that is, if

$$\phi^k < 1 \quad \text{and} \quad \Pi^k < \Pi^* \qquad (42)$$

or if

$$\phi^k > 1 \quad \text{and} \quad \Pi^k > \Pi^* \qquad (43)$$

We see that the position of ϕ^k with respect to 1, and thus the Taylor principle, still plays a central role for these equilibria.

5.6.2 Equilibria of Type $\mathcal{NR}$

For the steady state of type $\mathcal{NR}$ (definition 5.1) we have $\Pi = \Pi^*$. The associated characteristic polynomial is therefore

$$\Psi_{\mathcal{NR}}(\lambda) = (\lambda - \phi\kappa)(\lambda - 1) + (1 - \kappa)\lambda \qquad (44)$$

We can compute

$$\Psi_{\mathcal{NR}}(0) = \phi\kappa > 0 \tag{45}$$

$$\Psi_{\mathcal{NR}}(1) = 1 - \kappa \tag{46}$$

We see that the condition for local determinacy is

$$\kappa > 1 \tag{47}$$

We recognize it as the financial dominance (FD) condition that we described above (definition 5.2). The Taylor principle $\phi > 1$ is no longer the relevant criterion.

5.7 Non-Ricardian Dynamics: A Graphical Representation

We study in this section under what conditions global determinacy holds in a non-Ricardian environment. We will see that the Taylor principle is almost completely replaced by the "financial dominance" criterion defined in section 5.5, at least for the non-Ricardian equilibria. Ricardian equilibria (type $\mathcal{R}$) are studied in appendix B.

We will make extensive use below of graphical representations of the dynamic equations (25) and (26), so we begin with it.

From (25) the locus $X_{t+1} = X_t$ has actually two branches, whose equations are

$$X_t = 0 \quad \text{and} \quad \Pi_t = \Pi^*, \qquad \Pi^* = \frac{\gamma}{\zeta(1+n)} \tag{48}$$

From (26) the curve $\Pi_{t+1} = \Pi_t$ can be derived as

$$X_t = H(\Pi_t) \tag{49}$$

with

$$H(\Pi_t) = \frac{\Pi_t}{\nu\Pi^*} \left[\frac{\Phi(\Pi_t)}{\zeta} - \Pi_t \right] \tag{50}$$

We further note that the dynamic evolutions of X_t and Π_t are, respectively, characterized by (we restrict ourselves to $X_t \geq 0$ in what follows)

$$X_{t+1} > X_t \quad \text{if } \Pi_t < \Pi^* \tag{51}$$

$$\Pi_{t+1} > \Pi_t \quad \text{if } X_t < H(\Pi_t) \tag{52}$$

It will be useful in what follows to link satisfaction of the Taylor principle to the slope of the function H (equation 50). So we have:

Lemma 5.1 *Consider a potential equilibrium of type* $\mathcal{R}$, *denoted as* Π^k, *and corresponding to a point where the curve* $X_t = H(\Pi_t)$ *cuts the horizontal axis. At such a point:*

- *If the slope of H is negative, then* $\phi(\Pi^k) < 1$.
- *If the slope of H is positive, then* $\phi(\Pi^k) > 1$.

Proof Compute the derivative of H (equation 50) at the point Π^k. Using the fact that at equilibria of type $\mathcal{R}$, we have $\Phi(\Pi_t) = \xi\Pi_t$ we find

$$H'(\Pi^k) = \frac{\Pi^k}{\nu\Pi^*}[\phi(\Pi^k) - 1] \tag{53}$$

which trivially implies the result.   ∎

This relation between the curve H and the interest rate rule is illustrated in figure 5.2. The top panel of this figure repeats figure 5.1. There are two potential "Ricardian" equilibria, Π^1 and Π^2, which correspond to the intersection of the curve $\Phi(\Pi_t)/\xi$ with the 45 degree line. The Taylor principle is satisfied for Π^2 but not for Π^1. The lower panel shows the function H. The function H cuts the horizontal axis at Π^1 and Π^2, and in accordance with lemma 5.1, it slopes negatively at Π^1 and positively at Π^2.

5.8   Global Financial Dominance

We shall now see how the financial dominance criterion can ensure global determinacy. We will first consider, in the following proposition, the case where financial dominance holds for all values of the inflation rate.

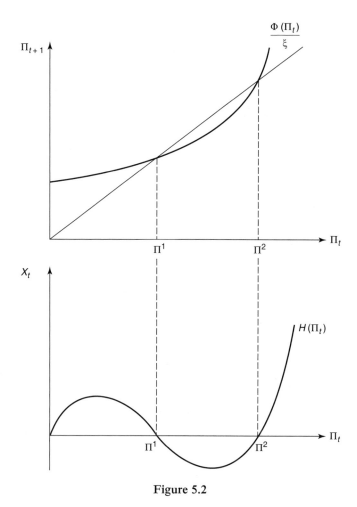

Figure 5.2

Proposition 5.1 *If the financial dominance criterion holds for all values of the inflation rate, that is, if*

$$\frac{\Phi(\Pi_t)}{\Pi_t} > \xi \qquad \forall \Pi_t \tag{54}$$

then there is a single globally determinate equilibrium of type $\mathcal{NR}$.

Proof We first see that under condition (54) there cannot be an equilibrium of type $\mathcal{R}$, since these equilibria are all characterized by $\Phi(\Pi) = \xi\Pi$. So there remains only the unique equilibrium Π^* of type $\mathcal{NR}$. Now, since

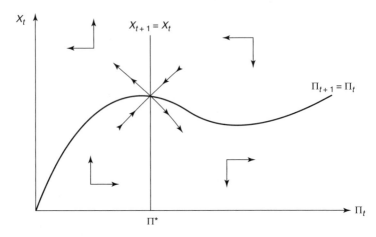

Figure 5.3

$\Phi(\Pi^*) > \xi\Pi^*$, we know from the results of section 5.6.2 that this equilibrium is characterized by saddle-point dynamics and is locally determinate.

Figure 5.3 depicts the two curves $X_{t+1} = X_t$ and $\Pi_{t+1} = \Pi_t$, as well as the dynamics of the economy given by (51) and (52), in the case corresponding to condition (54). It is easy to see from the dynamics depicted in figure 5.3 that this equilibrium is globally determinate.   ■

We may note that the preceding result does not depend on the elasticity of the function Φ as long as condition (54) applies. In other words, the Taylor principle is irrelevant for local or global determinacy when condition (54) holds.

5.9   Partial Financial Dominance

We now consider cases where the financial dominance criterion is not satisfied for all values of the inflation rate, and see that nevertheless this criterion still plays a central role in achieving global determinacy. Again we study in the next proposition equilibria of type $\mathcal{NR}$ (definition 5.1).

Proposition 5.2 *Consider an equilibrium of type $\mathcal{NR}$ characterized, in particular, by an inflation rate Π^* such that*

$$\frac{\Phi(\Pi^*)}{\Pi^*} > \xi \qquad (55)$$

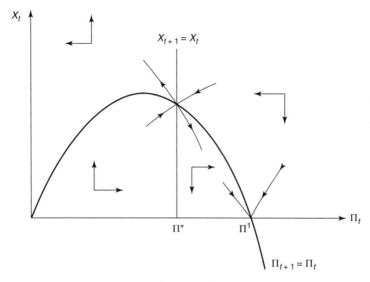

Figure 5.4

This equilibrium will be globally determinate if and only if

$$\frac{\Phi(\Pi_t)}{\Pi_t} > \xi \qquad \forall \Pi_t \geq \Pi^* \tag{56}$$

Proof We begin by showing that condition (56) is necessary. If condition (56) is not satisfied, then there must be a value $\Pi^1 > \Pi^*$ such that $\Phi(\Pi^1) = \xi \Pi^1$, meaning that Π^1 is an equilibrium of type $\mathcal{R}$. This is depicted in figure 5.4.

We see in figure 5.4 that the equilibrium Π^* is locally determinate but the equilibrium Π^1 is indeterminate. This is confirmed by the results of section 5.6.1 and lemma 5.1, which show that the two roots at equilibrium Π^1 are of a modulus smaller than 1. The dynamic system is thus globally indeterminate, and condition (56) is necessary.

We now show that condition (56) is sufficient for global determinacy. Recall that we studied the case where the curve $X_t = H(\Pi_t)$ is entirely above the horizontal axis (proposition 5.1). We study below cases where it intersects the horizontal axis.

Under condition (56) there cannot be a value $\Pi > \Pi^*$ such that $\Phi(\Pi) = \xi \Pi$. There can be, however, an even number of values $\Pi < \Pi^*$ which satisfy $\Phi(\Pi) = \xi \Pi$. Let us first consider the simplest case

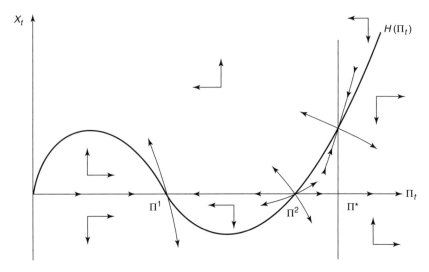

Figure 5.5

where there are two such values Π^1 and Π^2. This is represented in figure 5.5.

We see that we have one equilibrium of type $\mathcal{NR}$ corresponding to Π^*. This equilibrium displays saddle-path dynamics. But there are also two other potential equilibria, both of type $\mathcal{R}$, corresponding to the inflation rates Π^1 and Π^2. For the equilibrium Π^* to be globally determinate, we need these two other potential equilibria not to be reachable.

Let us first consider Π^1. The two roots, as we saw above (section 5.6.1), are $\phi(\Pi^1) < 1$, and $\Pi^*/\Pi^1 > 1$. We thus have saddle-path dynamics. The problem, however, is that the "converging branch" of this saddle-path dynamics is contained in the horizontal axis. So if $X_0 > 0$ (which we shall assume) this equilibrium will never be reached.

Let us now consider Π^2. The two roots are $\phi(\Pi^2) > 1$, and $\Pi^*/\Pi^2 > 1$. Since the two roots are of modulus greater than 1, this potential equilibrium will never be reached either.

To summarize, we have one equilibrium of type $\mathcal{NR}$ that displays saddle-path dynamics, and two potential equilibria of type $\mathcal{R}$ that cannot be reached. The equilibrium of type $\mathcal{NR}$ is globally determinate, as figure 5.5 clearly shows.

To be complete, we have to say what happens when there are more than two potential equilibria of type $\mathcal{R}$. Under condition (56) we have an even number K of such potential equilibria. It is easy to see (e.g., as in

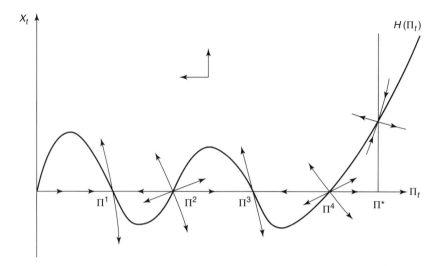

Figure 5.6

figure 5.6 where the case $K = 4$ is depicted) that potential equilibria with odd numbers have the same properties as Π^1 in figure 5.5, and potential equilibria with even numbers have the same properties as Π^2 in figure 5.5. So none of them can be reached, and the equilibrium of type $\mathcal{NR}$ is globally determinate. ∎

Proposition 5.2 tells us that what is important is that the FD condition be satisfied for "high" values of inflation. So if there is a danger of the real value of financial assets being driven to zero by high inflation, this condition ensures that agents will actually want to hold financial assets because their returns are attractive, and this will prevent a "collapse" of money and financial assets.

So we have proved that for achieving global determinacy of non-Ricardian equilibria the Taylor principle should be replaced by the financial dominance criterion. However, this could be an empty result if there was no function $\Phi(\Pi_t)$ such that the financial dominance criterion holds while the Taylor principle does not. We thus need to check below that there are functions $\Phi(\Pi_t)$ such that the Taylor principle is not satisfied, and nevertheless condition (54) is satisfied.[4]

---

4. In such a case the weaker condition (56) is a fortiori satisfied.

5.10   Interest Rate Rules and Global Determinacy: Examples

We will now give two simple examples of interest rate rules where the Taylor principle does not hold, at least in the vicinity of the long-run equilibrium. Nevertheless, global determinacy can obtain in both examples because the financial dominance criterion is satisfied.

5.10.1   A Linear Rule

First we study some simple linear interest rate rules:

$$\Phi(\Pi_t) = A\Pi_t + B, \qquad A > 0,\ B > 1 \tag{57}$$

Consider the function

$$\Phi(\Pi_t) - \xi\Pi_t = A\Pi_t + B - \xi\Pi_t \tag{58}$$

If this function is positive for all values of Π_t, in view of proposition 5.1, there is global determinacy. A sufficient condition for this is that

$$A > \xi \tag{59}$$

Let us compute the elasticity of this interest rate rule:

$$\phi(\Pi_t) = \frac{\partial \log \Phi(\Pi_t)}{\partial \log \Pi_t} = \frac{\partial \log(A\Pi_t + B)}{\partial \log \Pi_t} = \frac{A\Pi_t}{A\Pi_t + B} < 1 \tag{60}$$

This elasticity is always smaller than 1. If the parameter A satisfies (59) global determinacy will be achieved with $\phi < 1$.

5.10.2   Local Interest Rate Pegging

Next we consider an interest rate rule that is "inactive" for a range of the inflation rate:

$$\Phi(\Pi_t) = (1 + i_0) \max\left[1, \left(\frac{\Pi_t}{\Pi_0}\right)^{\varepsilon}\right] \tag{61}$$

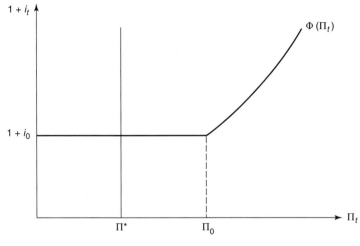

Figure 5.7

This interest rate rule has two branches (figure 5.7). For $\Pi_t \leq \Pi_0$, the rule is inactive and the interest rate is pegged at i_0. For values of inflation above Π_0, the rule becomes active.

Let us consider again the function

$$\Phi(\Pi_t) - \xi\Pi_t = (1 + i_0) \max\left[1, \left(\frac{\Pi_t}{\Pi_0}\right)^{\varepsilon}\right] - \xi\Pi_t \tag{62}$$

In order to apply proposition 5.1, we want this function to be positive for all values of Π_t. First one shifts from one branch of this function to the other at $\Pi_t = \Pi_0$. The value of (62) at this intersection must be positive, so we must have

$$1 + i_0 > \xi\Pi_0 \tag{63}$$

Furthermore, for (62) to be positive for large values of Π_t, we should have $\varepsilon \geq 1$. It is easy to see that the conjunction of (63) and $\varepsilon \geq 1$ ensures that (62) will be positive for all values of Π_t and thus, by proposition 5.1, that we have global determinacy.

Now the long-run equilibrium is at

$$\Pi^* = \frac{\gamma}{\zeta(1 + n)} \tag{64}$$

We would like this long-run equilibrium Π^* to be in the zone where monetary policy is "inactive," namely where $\Pi_t < \Pi_0$ (figure 5.7). This will be achieved if (by condition 63)

$$\Pi^* = \frac{\gamma}{\zeta(1+n)} < \Pi_0 < \frac{1+i_0}{\xi} \tag{65}$$

From (65) it will be possible to choose an adequate Π_0 if

$$\frac{(1+n)(1+i_0)\zeta}{\gamma} > \xi \tag{66}$$

In this formula $\gamma/(1+n)\zeta$ is the inflation rate in steady state, and the left-hand side is thus the real rate of interest on financial assets. So condition (66) is simply a way to say that the financial dominance condition is satisfied at the long-run equilibrium.

5.11   Conclusions

We examined in this chapter conditions under which interest rate rules achieve global determinacy in non-Ricardian economies. We identified two types of equilibria, each with distinct determinacy conditions.

The first type of equilibrium (type $\mathcal{R}$) was called Ricardian. These equilibria look very much like equilibria in a Ricardian economy. Not surprisingly, in such equilibria the global determinacy conditions are similar to those in a pure Ricardian economy, that is, the Taylor principle supplemented by conditions on the growth of assets so that only the potential equilibrium with the highest inflation rate is feasible (appendix B).

Things change radically for the second type of equilibria, the non-Ricardian (type $\mathcal{NR}$) equilibria. There financial assets have real value, and the real interest rate is different from the autarkic rate. In such equilibria a central global determinacy condition appears to be the financial dominance criterion, which basically says that through the nominal interest rate rule, the real interest rate should be maintained at a value superior to the autarkic real interest rate. This way households are willing to hold financial assets, and the total value of these assets gives the "nominal anchor" that will pin down the price level.

5.12   References

This chapter is adapted from Bénassy and Guillard (2005).

The issue of global determinacy under interest rate rules in Ricardian economies is notably studied in Benhabib, Schmitt-Grohe, and Uribe (2001a, b, 2002) and Woodford (1999, 2003).

The financial dominance criterion appears initially in Wallace (1980) for an OLG economy where money is the single store of value. It is extended in Bénassy (2005) for economies with both money and bonds.

Appendix A: Global Determinacy in Ricardian Economies

We demonstrate here the determinacy conditions that we presented in section 5.3.2.

Proposition 5.3   *Denote as* $\Pi^1, \ldots, \Pi^k, \ldots, \Pi^K$ *potential equilibria in a Ricardian economy, that is, the solutions in* Π *to the equation*

$$\frac{\Phi(\Pi)}{\Pi} = \xi \tag{67}$$

Then the equilibrium Π^K *is globally determinate if*

$$\phi(\Pi^K) > 1 \tag{68}$$

$$\Pi^{K-1} < \Pi^* < \Pi^K \tag{69}$$

with

$$\Pi^* = \frac{\gamma}{\zeta} \tag{70}$$

Proof   Let us recall the dynamic system

$$\Pi_{t+1} = \frac{\Phi(\Pi_t)}{\xi} \tag{71}$$

$$X_{t+1} = \Pi^* \frac{X_t}{\Pi_t} \tag{72}$$

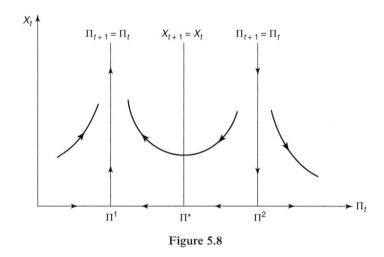

Figure 5.8

We will use a graphical argument for $K = 2$. Figure 5.8 shows in the (Π_t, X_t) plane a case with two equilibria Π^1 and Π^2 where conditions (68) and (69) are satisfied. The locus $\Pi_{t+1} = \Pi_t$ consists of the two vertical lines $\Pi_t = \Pi^1$ and $\Pi_t = \Pi^2$, whereas the locus $X_{t+1} = X_t$ consists of the vertical $\Pi_t = \Pi^*$.

Figure 5.8 shows that clearly the equilibrium Π^2 is globally stable. If we draw the same picture with either $\Pi^* < \Pi^1$ or $\Pi^* > \Pi^2$, it is easy to see that there is no globally stable equilibrium. Finally this argument extends easily to $K > 2$, and this is left to the reader.   ∎

Appendix B: Global Determinacy: Equilibria of Type $\mathcal{R}$

When we studied non-Ricardian economies in the main body of this chapter, we concentrated on the global determinacy of non-Ricardian equilibria, called equilibria of type $\mathcal{NR}$, because these equilibria were the main novelty of the analysis of this chapter.

But, as we pointed out, these equilibria are not the only possible equilibria. We identified another type of equilibria, "Ricardian equilibria" (i.e., equilibria of type $\mathcal{R}$), whose properties are closer to those encountered in Ricardian economies.

In order to be complete, we will study in this appendix conditions under which these Ricardian equilibria are globally determinate. Such a case appears in figure 5.9, where it is assumed that the curve $H(\Pi_t)$ cuts the horizontal axis twice, in Π^1 and Π^2.

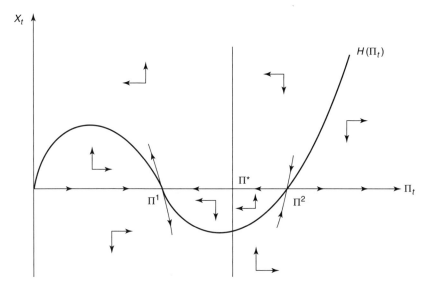

Figure 5.9

Proposition 5.4 *Denote as* $\Pi^1, \ldots, \Pi^k, \ldots, \Pi^K$ *potential equilibria of type $\mathcal{R}$, that is, the solutions in Π to the equation*

$$\frac{\Phi(\Pi)}{\Pi} = \zeta \tag{73}$$

Then the equilibrium Π^K is globally determinate if

$$\phi(\Pi^K) > 1 \tag{74}$$

$$\Pi^{K-1} < \Pi^* < \Pi^K \tag{75}$$

with

$$\Pi^* = \frac{\gamma}{(1+n)\zeta} \tag{76}$$

Proof Under condition (74) there is an even number of potential equilibria. The only possible globally determinate equilibrium is that corresponding to the highest inflation rate, which is $k = K$. Let us consider first the situation (figure 5.9) where there are two such equilibria of type $\mathcal{R}$, Π^1 and Π^2, where the curve $X_t = H(X_t)$ intersects the horizontal axis,

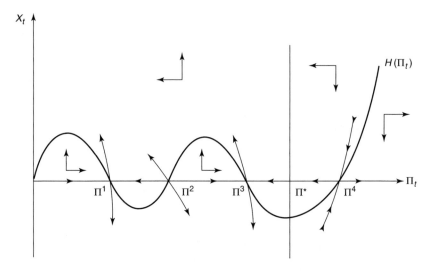

Figure 5.10

and where (condition 75)

$$\Pi^1 < \Pi^* < \Pi^2 \tag{77}$$

We want to show that the equilibrium corresponding to Π^2 is locally and globally determinate.

Consider first Π^2. By lemma 5.1, one root is $\phi(\Pi^2) > 1$. The other root, from section 5.6.1, is $\Pi^*/\Pi^2 < 1$. We thus have saddle-path dynamics.

Let us now consider the other potential equilibrium Π^1. By lemma 5.1, one root is equal to $\phi(\Pi^1) < 1$. The other root, from section 5.6.1, is $\Pi^*/\Pi^1 > 1$. We have saddle-path dynamics, but because the converging branch is contained in the horizontal axis, if $X_0 > 0$ that equilibrium cannot be reached. As a consequence Π^2 is globally determinate.

Finally let us consider the more general case of an even number K of potential equilibria of type $\mathcal{R}$. Figure 5.10 depicts the case $K = 4$.

We see that potential equilibria with an odd number have the same properties as the potential equilibrium Π^1 in figure 5.9, and cannot be reached. As for potential equilibria of even number k (except K), they are characterized by two roots $\phi(\Pi^k) > 1$ (by lemma 5.1) and $\Pi^*/\Pi^k > 1$ (from section 5.6.1). With both roots of modulus bigger than 1, they cannot be reached either.

Finally Π^K has saddle-path dynamics and is globally determinate. ∎

We may note that the conditions for global determinacy of these equilibria are very close to those that we encountered in the case of Ricardian economies (appendix A).

Appendix C: Transversality Conditions

We devote this appendix to the transversality conditions in both Ricardian and non-Ricardian economies.[5] We will see that (1) for non-Ricardian equilibria the transversality conditions are always satisfied and (2) for Ricardian equilibria the global determinacy conditions that we derived in propositions 5.3 and 5.4 are sufficient for the transversality conditions to be satisfied as well.

Ricardian Economies

Without population growth, the representative household's transversality condition is given by

$$\lim_{t \to \infty} D_t \Omega_t = 0 \tag{78}$$

where

$$D_t = \prod_{s=0}^{t-1} \frac{1}{1 + i_s} \tag{79}$$

At a stationary equilibrium, $1 + i = \xi \Pi$ and condition (78) is equivalent to

$$\lim_{t \to \infty} \left(\frac{\gamma}{\xi \Pi} \right)^t \Omega_0 = 0 \tag{80}$$

For $\Omega_0 \neq 0$, which we will assume, this equation is verified if and only if

$$\gamma < \xi \Pi \tag{81}$$

---

5. The importance of transversality conditions for the issue of global determinacy in Ricardian models is emphasized by Benhabib, Schmitt-Grohe, and Uribe (2002) and Woodford (1999, 2003).

To apply condition (81), consider the case represented in figure 5.1, with two potential equilibria. We want the equilibrium Π^2 to satisfy the above transversality condition. But we saw (in proposition 5.3) that a condition for global determinacy of Π^2 is

$$\Pi^1 < \Pi^* < \Pi^2 \tag{82}$$

with

$$\Pi^* = \frac{\gamma}{\zeta} \tag{83}$$

Therefore, if the global determinacy condition (82) is satisfied, the transversality condition (81) is also satisfied for Π^2 since $\xi = \zeta/\beta$.

More generally, we have seen (proposition 5.3) that if there are K solutions, $\Pi^1, \ldots, \Pi^k, \ldots, \Pi^K$, to the equation $\Phi(\Pi) = \xi\Pi$, then Π^K is globally determinate if

$$\phi(\Pi^K) > 1 \tag{84}$$

$$\Pi^{K-1} < \Pi^* < \Pi^K \tag{85}$$

and this implies that the transversality condition is satisfied for the equilibrium corresponding to the highest inflation Π^K.

Non-Ricardian Economies

We will now see that the transversality condition is always satisfied at non-Ricardian equilibria. For Ricardian equilibria, global determinacy is a sufficient condition for the satisfaction of the transversality condition.

With population growth, the transversality condition becomes:

$$\lim_{t \to \infty} \frac{D_t \Omega_t}{N_t} = 0 \tag{86}$$

again with $D_t = [(1 + i_0) \ldots (1 + i_{t-1})]^{-1}$. For stationary equilibria, using (22), (86) is equivalent to

$$\lim_{t \to \infty} \left[\frac{\gamma}{(1 + n)(1 + i)} \right]^t \left(\frac{\Omega_0}{N_0} \right) = 0 \tag{87}$$

For $\Omega_0 \neq 0$, this equation is verified if and only if

$$\gamma < (1+n)(1+i) \tag{88}$$

We must distinguish two cases.

1. For the steady state of type $\mathcal{NR}$, from (31) we have

$$\Pi^* = \frac{\gamma}{\zeta(1+n)}, \quad \Phi(\Pi^*) = 1 + i^* > \xi\Pi^* \tag{89}$$

Putting the two together, we obtain

$$\beta(1+n)(1+i^*) > \gamma \tag{90}$$

which implies (88). So the tranversality condition is always satisfied in a non-Ricardian ($\mathcal{NR}$) equilibrium.

2. For steady states of type $\mathcal{R}$, the gross real rate of interest is equal to ξ. So $1 + i = \xi\Pi$ and (88) becomes

$$\frac{\gamma}{(1+n)\xi} < \Pi \tag{91}$$

We saw above (proposition 5.4) that for equilibria of type $\mathcal{R}$ one condition for global determinacy is

$$\Pi^{K-1} < \Pi^* < \Pi^K \tag{92}$$

We see that if this condition is satisfied, then the transversality condition (91) is automatically satisfied for Π^K, since

$$\Pi^* = \frac{\gamma}{\zeta(1+n)} \tag{93}$$

6

Fiscal Policy and Determinacy

6.1 Introduction

In the two previous chapters we studied how adequate conditions on monetary policies lead to price determinacy. But of course fiscal policy is also most important, and we devote this chapter to an investigation of the relation between fiscal policy and determinacy.

In fact in the recent years a challenging theory of price determinacy in monetary economies has developed, the fiscal theory of the price level (FTPL). What the FTPL says is that even in circumstances where monetary policy is not sufficient to bring determinacy, as in the case of a pure interest rate peg, adequate fiscal policies can restore determinacy. The fiscal policies that achieve determinacy are such that the government's intertemporal budget constraint is not balanced in all circumstances. In fact the intuition behind the theory is that unless one starts from a particular price level, the government's real liabilities will explode in time. The problem with the FTPL is that the corresponding fiscal policies are rather adventurous because the government does not plan on balancing the budget in every circumstance, and this can lead in many situations to explosive real liabilities. These controversial policy implications have led to numerous contributions and a heated debate.

Our purpose in this chapter is to show that the controversial policy implications of FTPL are actually due to the particular "Ricardian" framework whithin which the results were derived. Indeed it will become evident that in moving to a "non-Ricardian" framework the results are much less controversial. In particular, in the non-Ricardian framework, price determinacy, whether local or global, is consistent with much more reasonable fiscal policies.

6.2   The Model

Again we use the model described in chapter 2, section 2.2, but have to be more explicit on monetary and fiscal policies.

6.2.1   Monetary Policy

In what follows we study two types of monetary policies. First, and since we want to concentrate on the effects of fiscal policy, we consider again a simple policy of interest rate pegging, which is the typical situation where the FTPL holds. To simplify the exposition, we assume that the pegged interest rate is constant in time so that

$$i_t = i_0 \qquad \forall t \tag{1}$$

We then follow with a study of more general policies where, as in the previous chapter, the nominal interest rate responds to inflation as

$$1 + i_t = \Phi(\Pi_t), \qquad \Phi(\Pi_t) \geq 1 \tag{2}$$

with $\Pi_t = P_t/P_{t-1}$.

6.2.2   Fiscal Policy

If the budget was balanced, taxes would be equal to interest payments on bonds:

$$P_t T_t = i_t B_t \tag{3}$$

Since fiscal policy is our point of interest in this chapter, we want to include more general fiscal policies. So we assume here that the government has policies of the form

$$P_t T_t = i_t B_t + (1 - \gamma)\Omega_t + \delta P_t Y_t, \qquad \gamma \geq 0, \delta \geq 0 \tag{4}$$

As compared to the balanced budget policy (3) two terms are added: the term $\delta P_t Y_t$, which says that the governement taxes a fraction δ of national income, and the term $(1 - \gamma)\Omega_t$, which says that the government may want to withdraw a fraction $1 - \gamma$ of its outstanding financial liabilities. If γ is greater than 1, it actually corresponds to an expansion of government liabilities. The FTPL, as we will see, corresponds notably to a "large" value of γ.

6.3   The Dynamic Equations

Recall the government budget equation

$$\Omega_{t+1} = (1 + i_t)\Omega_t - i_t M_t - P_t T_t \tag{5}$$

In combining (4) and (5) with $\Omega_t = M_t + B_t$, we find

$$\Omega_{t+1} = \gamma\Omega_t - \delta P_t Y_t \tag{6}$$

Turning now to nominal income $P_t Y_t$, it was shown in proposition 2.1, chapter 2, that, assuming $N_{t+1}/N_t = 1 + n$, its dynamics is given by

$$P_{t+1} Y_{t+1} = \beta(1 + n)(1 + i_t)P_t Y_t - (1 - \beta)n\Omega_{t+1} \tag{7}$$

Combining this with equation (2), we obtain

$$P_{t+1} Y_{t+1} = \beta(1 + n)P_t Y_t \Phi(\Pi_t) - (1 - \beta)n\Omega_{t+1} \tag{8}$$

Equations (6) and (8) are the basic dynamic equations of our model. To contrast our later results with the traditional ones, we first examine as a benchmark some determinacy conditions in the traditional Ricardian case.

6.4   Ricardian Economies and Determinacy

6.4.1   Dynamics

To obtain the traditional Ricardian version of the model, it is enough to take $n = 0$. Equation (8) is then rewritten as

$$P_{t+1} Y_{t+1} = \beta P_t Y_t \Phi(\Pi_t) \tag{9}$$

As in chapter 5, we set Π_t and the predetermined variable $X_t = \Omega_t / P_{t-1} Y_{t-1}$ as our working variables. The dynamic system (6), (9) is then rewritten as

$$\Pi_{t+1} = \frac{\Phi(\Pi_t)}{\xi} \tag{10}$$

$$X_{t+1} = \frac{\gamma X_t}{\zeta \Pi_t} - \delta \tag{11}$$

Steady states (Π, X) of this system (when they exist) are characterized by

$$\Pi = \frac{\Phi(\Pi)}{\xi} \tag{12}$$

$$X = \frac{\gamma X}{\zeta \Pi} - \delta \tag{13}$$

We will assume that the system (12), (13) admits at least one steady state. Linearizing (10) and (11) around it, we find

$$\begin{bmatrix} \Pi_{t+1} - \Pi \\ X_{t+1} - X \end{bmatrix} = \begin{bmatrix} \phi & 0 \\ -\gamma X / \zeta \Pi^2 & \gamma / \zeta \Pi \end{bmatrix} \begin{bmatrix} \Pi_t - \Pi \\ X_t - X \end{bmatrix} \tag{14}$$

with

$$\phi = \phi(\Pi) = \frac{\Pi \Phi'(\Pi)}{\Phi(\Pi)} \tag{15}$$

The two roots are thus ϕ and $\gamma / \zeta \Pi$.

6.4.2 Fiscal Policies and Local Determinacy

The variable X_t is predetermined, whereas Π_t is not. So local determinacy is obtained if one root has modulus greater than 1. This gives us two possibilities for local determinacy. The first is

$$\phi > 1, \quad \gamma < \zeta \Pi \tag{16}$$

The first inequality in (16) is the Taylor principle, which we previously studied. Note that this Taylor principle is combined with a "prudent" fiscal policy that puts an upper bound on γ, the coefficient of expansion of government liabilities.

However, we see that with the more general tax function, a new possibility appears for local determinacy, and it corresponds to the FTPL:

$$\phi < 1, \quad \gamma > \zeta \Pi \tag{17}$$

The condition $\phi < 1$ says that the Taylor principle is not satisfied. The condition $\gamma > \zeta \Pi$ means that the coefficient γ, which somehow measures the "target" expansion of government liabilities, must be higher than $\zeta \Pi$. Since $\zeta \Pi$ is the rate of growth of nominal income, this will imply, in particular, that the ratio of government liabilities to income will be explosive. Clearly, this is not a very reasonable fiscal policy.

6.4.3 An Interest Rate Peg

To see this point even more clearly, let us consider the particular case of an interest rate peg:

$$\Phi(\Pi_t) = 1 + i_0 \tag{18}$$

The dynamic system becomes

$$\Omega_{t+1} = \gamma \Omega_t - \delta P_t Y_t \tag{19}$$

$$P_{t+1} Y_{t+1} = \beta(1 + i_0) P_t Y_t \tag{20}$$

Combining (19) and (20), we find the dynamics of $\Omega_t / P_t Y_t$:

$$\frac{\Omega_{t+1}}{P_{t+1} Y_{t+1}} = \frac{\gamma}{\beta(1 + i_0)} \frac{\Omega_t}{P_t Y_t} - \frac{\delta}{\beta(1 + i_0)} \tag{21}$$

This is represented in figure 6.1. The condition for determinacy is

$$\gamma > \beta(1 + i_0) \tag{22}$$

Combining (21) and (22), we see that in order to achieve determinacy, the parameter γ must be chosen high enough so that the ratio of

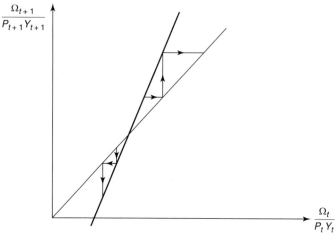

Figure 6.1

government liabilities to income is explosive. This is clearly a highly adventurous policy.

From (21) we can also compute the steady state value of $\Omega_t / P_t Y_t$:

$$\frac{\Omega_t}{P_t Y_t} = \frac{\delta}{\gamma - \beta(1 + i_0)} > 0 \tag{23}$$

We finally note that condition (22) is a particular case of condition (17), since under the interest rate peg (18) we have, using (12) and $\xi = \zeta/\beta$,

$$\zeta \Pi = \beta(1 + i_0) \tag{24}$$

6.5   Local Determinacy in the Non-Ricardian Case

We will now move to a non-Ricardian framework, and we want to show that at least for equilibia of the $\mathcal{NR}$ type, adventurous fiscal policies like (17) or (22) are no longer necessary for determinacy. More precisely, we will study a case that admits equilibria of both types identified in the previous chapter, $\mathcal{R}$ and $\mathcal{NR}$. We will see that although the determinacy conditions of equilibria of type $\mathcal{R}$ are similar to those of the FTPL, the conditions for equilibria of type $\mathcal{NR}$ imply much more reasonable fiscal policies.

We will study in this section local determinacy, leaving global determinacy to the next section. In order to make the comparison with the Ricardian case particularly transparent, we will continue to concentrate on the case of an interest rate peg $\Phi(\Pi_t) = 1 + i_0$. We will further assume $\delta = 0$. The dynamic system (6) and (8) then becomes

$$\Omega_{t+1} = \gamma\Omega_t \tag{25}$$

$$P_{t+1}Y_{t+1} = \beta(1+n)(1+i_0)P_tY_t - (1-\beta)n\Omega_{t+1} \tag{26}$$

or, in terms of the variables Π_t and X_t,

$$X_{t+1} = \Pi^* \frac{X_t}{\Pi_t} \tag{27}$$

$$\Pi_{t+1} = \frac{1+i_0}{\zeta} - v\Pi^* \frac{X_t}{\Pi_t} \tag{28}$$

with

$$\Pi^* = \frac{\gamma}{\zeta(1+n)}, \quad v = \frac{(1-\beta)n}{(1+n)\zeta} \tag{29}$$

Steady states of the system (Π, X) are given by

$$X = \Pi^* \frac{X}{\Pi} \tag{30}$$

$$\Pi = \frac{1+i_0}{\zeta} - v\Pi^* \frac{X}{\Pi} \tag{31}$$

Here we see that there are two steady states, one of type $\mathcal{R}$ (Π^1) and one of type $\mathcal{NR}$ (Π^*):

$$X^1 = 0, \quad \Pi^1 = \frac{1+i_0}{\zeta}, \qquad \text{Type } \mathcal{R} \tag{32}$$

$$\Pi = \Pi^*, \quad X^* = \frac{1}{v}\left(\frac{1+i_0}{\zeta} - \Pi^*\right), \qquad \text{Type } \mathcal{NR} \tag{33}$$

Let us linearize (27) and (28) around these steady states. We obtain

$$\begin{bmatrix} \Pi_{t+1} - \Pi \\ X_{t+1} - X \end{bmatrix} = \begin{bmatrix} vX/\Pi & -v\Pi^*/\Pi \\ -X/\Pi & \Pi^*/\Pi \end{bmatrix} \begin{bmatrix} \Pi_t - \Pi \\ X_t - X \end{bmatrix} \tag{34}$$

The characteristic polynomial is

$$\Psi(\lambda) = \lambda^2 - \left(\frac{vX}{\Pi} + \frac{\Pi^*}{\Pi} \right) \lambda \tag{35}$$

The roots are 0 and $(vX + \Pi^*)/\Pi$, so the condition for local determinacy is

$$\frac{vX}{\Pi} + \frac{\Pi^*}{\Pi} > 1 \tag{36}$$

Let us now investigate successively this condition for the two types of equilibria. For the equilibrium of type $\mathcal{R}$, $X = 0$, so condition (36) boils down to

$$\Pi^* > \Pi^1 \tag{37}$$

or, in view of (29) and (32), and since $\xi = \zeta/\beta$,

$$\gamma > \beta(1 + n)(1 + i_0) = \theta \tag{38}$$

Note that this condition is very similar to the "FTPL" condition (22), and it similarly calls for a "large" expansion of government's liabilities.

Let us now consider the equilibrium of type $\mathcal{NR}$. There $\Pi = \Pi^*$, so condition (36) boils down to

$$X > 0 \tag{39}$$

or, in view of (33) and the definition of Π^* (equation 29),

$$\gamma < \beta(1 + n)(1 + i_0) = \theta \tag{40}$$

We see that this is the opposite of (38)! This time the condition for local stability is that the coefficient of fiscal expansion be *lower* than a given value, not higher, as in equations (22) or (38).

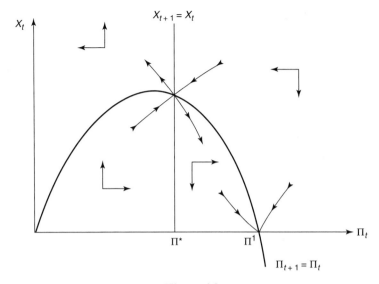

Figure 6.2

We can represent the dynamics in the (Π_t, X_t) plane (figure 6.2). Condition (40) implies that the vertical $\Pi_t = \Pi^*$ is to the left of the intersection of the curve $\Pi_{t+1} = \Pi_t$ with the horizontal axis so that the dynamic system looks as it does in figure 6.2.

Nevertheless, despite our finding that the non-Ricardian equilibrium can be locally determinate under reasonable fiscal policies, the system as a whole is indeterminate (figure 6.2). So we next take a look at the problem of global determinacy.

6.6 Global Determinacy

We want to show here that we can achieve not only local but also global determinacy without having to implement adventurous fiscal policies. Recall from section 6.4 that in the Ricardian framework there are two alternative conditions for price determinacy, the Taylor principle and the FTPL. Our objective is to show that in a non-Ricardian world it is possible to obtain global determinacy even though neither of these two conditions is satisfied. We have already treated implicitly the case $\delta = 0$ in the previous chapter (propositions 5.1 and 5.2), so we will now investigate sufficient conditions for global determinacy when $\delta > 0$.

Proposition 6.1   *Assume $\delta > 0$, and that the monetary policy satisfies*

$$\phi(\Pi_t) < 1 \tag{41}$$

$$\frac{\Phi(\Pi_t)}{\Pi_t} > \xi \tag{42}$$

Then there is a single globally determinate equilibrium of type $\mathcal{NR}$.

Proof   From (6) and (8) we deduce the dynamic system in Π_t and X_t:

$$X_{t+1} = \Pi^* \frac{X_t}{\Pi_t} - \delta \tag{43}$$

$$\Pi_{t+1} = \frac{\Phi(\Pi_t)}{\xi} + \delta v - v\Pi^* \frac{X_t}{\Pi_t} \tag{44}$$

where the expressions of Π^* and v are as given in equation (29).
   The curve $X_{t+1} = X_t$ is expressed by

$$X_t = \frac{\delta\Pi_t}{\Pi^* - \Pi_t} \tag{45}$$

The curve $\Pi_{t+1} = \Pi_t$ is expressed by

$$X_t = \frac{\Pi_t}{v\Pi^*}\left[\frac{\Phi(\Pi_t)}{\xi} - \Pi_t + \delta v\right] \tag{46}$$

First, note that under condition (42) (the financial dominance criterion) the $\Pi_{t+1} = \Pi_t$ curve is entirely above the horizontal axis. Second, note that the derivatives at the origin for the curves $X_{t+1} = X_t$ and $\Pi_{t+1} = \Pi_t$ are respectively

$$\frac{\delta}{\Pi^*} \quad \text{and} \quad \frac{\delta}{\Pi^*} + \frac{\Phi(0)}{v\xi\Pi^*} \tag{47}$$

so that the at the origin the curve $\Pi_{t+1} = \Pi_t$ is always above the curve $X_{t+1} = X_t$ as in figure 6.3.

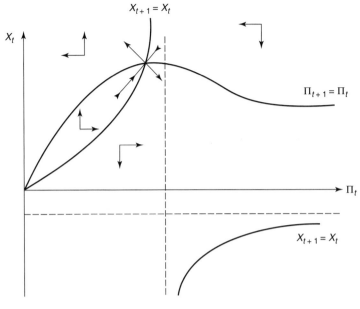

Figure 6.3

To establish global determinacy, we first check that, as in figure 6.3, the two curves $X_{t+1} = X_t$ and $\Pi_{t+1} = \Pi_t$ have a unique intersection. In view of (45) and (46) the potential intersections are given by the solutions to the equation

$$\frac{\delta \Pi_t}{\Pi^* - \Pi_t} = \frac{\Pi_t}{v \Pi^*} \left[\frac{\Phi(\Pi_t)}{\xi} - \Pi_t + \delta v \right] \tag{48}$$

After we divide by Π_t and subtract δ / Π^* from both sides, (48) becomes

$$\frac{\delta \Pi_t}{\Pi^* - \Pi_t} = \frac{1}{v} \left[\frac{\Phi(\Pi_t)}{\xi} - \Pi_t \right] \tag{49}$$

The left-hand and right-hand sides of (49) are represented in figure 6.4.

A sufficient condition for a unique intersection is that the derivative of the left-hand side of (49) be larger than the derivative of the right-hand side at a potential intersection point. The condition is thus

$$\frac{\delta \Pi^*}{(\Pi^* - \Pi_t)^2} > \frac{1}{v} \left[\frac{\Phi'(\Pi_t)}{\xi} - 1 \right] \tag{50}$$

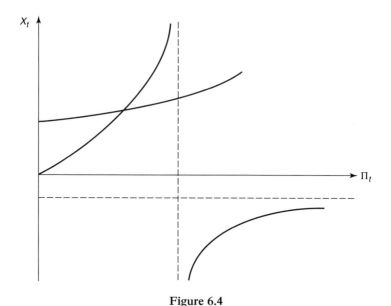

Figure 6.4

Using (49) (which is verified at an intersection point), we rewrite this condition as

$$\frac{\Pi^*}{\Pi^* - \Pi_t}\left[\frac{\Phi(\Pi_t)}{\xi} - \Pi_t\right] > \Pi_t\left[\frac{\Phi'(\Pi_t)}{\xi} - 1\right] \tag{51}$$

Since the first fraction of the left-hand side is bigger than one, a sufficient condition is

$$\frac{\Phi(\Pi_t)}{\xi} - \Pi_t > \Pi_t\left[\frac{\Phi'(\Pi_t)}{\xi} - 1\right] \tag{52}$$

or

$$\frac{\Pi_t\Phi'(\Pi_t)}{\Phi'(\Pi_t)} < 1 \tag{53}$$

which is condition (41). So we see that if the interest rate rule does not satisfy the Taylor principle, the intersection is unique, as in figures 6.3 and 6.4. Now figure 6.3 depicts the global dynamics of the system, and we see that the unique steady state is globally determinate.   ∎

Of course, we must check that there exist functions $\Phi(\Pi_t)$ such that the Taylor principle does not hold (condition 41) and the financial dominance holds (condition 42). We saw such functions in the preceding chapter, and notably the simple linear rules

$$\Phi(\Pi_t) = A\Pi_t + B, \qquad A \geq \xi, B > 1 \tag{54}$$

which are the rules in section 5.10.2 above.

6.7 Conclusions

We have seen that in the Ricardian case, if the Taylor principle is not satisfied, price determinacy can nevertheless obtain if the fiscal authority expands government liabilities at such a high rate that these liabilities become explosive (e.g., see conditions 17 or 22). This is a central mechanism behind the fiscal theory of the price level.

This controversial prescription is not any longer necessary in a non-Ricardian world. We found indeed that in such a case an explosive expansion of government liabilities is not a requisite for local or global price determinacy of non-Ricardian equilibria, and that price determinacy can be associated to very reasonable fiscal prescriptions (e.g., see condition 40). Finally we saw that global determinacy can be achieved with a combination of monetary and fiscal policies where monetary policy does not satisfy the "Taylor principle" and fiscal policies can be "reasonable" (proposition 6.1).

So it appears that the controversial policy prescriptions associated with the FTPL are linked with the Ricardian character of the economies in which they were derived. Such policy prescriptions are no longer necessary when we move to a (more realistic) non-Ricardian framework.

6.8 References

This chapter is adapted from Bénassy (2004).

The fiscal theory of the price level comes notably from the works of Leeper (1991), Sims (1994), and Woodford (1994, 1995). Explicitations and criticisms are found notably in Buiter (2002), Kocherlakota and Phelan (1999), McCallum (2001), Niepelt (2004), and Weil (2002).

Part III

Optimal Policy

7

A Simple Framework for Policy Analysis

7.1 Introduction

In this and the next three chapters we study a number of optimal policy issues. As we indicated in the introduction to this book, it turns out for some of the questions we investigate below that the Weil model of the preceding chapters can sometimes lead to calculations that are too complex. So we will use another non-Ricardian model, a simple overlapping generations model that generalizes the OLG model of chapter 1 to include work and production.

Before developing more specific themes, we will in this chapter describe the basic model and the associated optimality criterion. Since in the subsequent chapters we will study this model under Walrasian market clearing and under price and wage rigidities, we will derive a number of general equilibrium equations that apply to all these cases. Finally, as a benchmark, we will study optimal policy in a Walrasian setting.

7.2 The Model

We will use a monetary overlapping generations model (Samuelson 1958) with production. The economy includes representative firms and households, and the government.

7.2.1 The Agents

Each household lives for two periods. Households born in period t work L_t and consume C_{1t} in period t, consume C_{2t+1} in period $t+1$. They save from one period to the next through financial assets. Households of generation t maximize the expected value of their utility U_t, with

$$U_t = \alpha_t \log C_{1t} + \log C_{2t+1} - (1 + \alpha_t) L_t \qquad (1)$$

where the α_t's are positive stochastic variables whose variations represent demand shocks, since, as we will see below, the propensity to consume in period t is equal to $\alpha_t/(1 + \alpha_t)$. The coefficient $1 + \alpha_t$ in the disutility of labor is chosen so as to yield a constant Walrasian labor supply in the absence of government intervention (see section 7.5 below). This way variations in α_t have the characteristics of pure demand shocks.

As in the previous chapters we denote as Ω_t the total amount of financial assets that agents hold at the beginning of period t. Since young households are born with no assets, these assets are entirely in the hands of old households.

Households are submitted in each period of their life to a cash in advance constraint. These are written for the household born in period t:

$$M_{1t} \geq P_t C_{1t}, \quad M_{2t+1} \geq P_{t+1} C_{2t+1} \qquad (2)$$

The young household, who starts life without any financial asset, will need to borrow money in order to satisfy this cash in advance constraint. It can do so at the interest rate i_t set by the government. The total quantity of money is simply $M_t = M_{1t} + M_{2t}$.

The representative firm in period t has a production function

$$Y_t = Z_t L_t \qquad (3)$$

where Y_t is output, L_t is labor input, and Z_t is a technology shock common to all firms. Firms belong to the young households, to which they distribute their profits, if any. To make the exposition simpler, we will assume that the two shocks, α_t and Z_t, are stochastic i.i.d. variables.

7.2.2 Government Policies and Information

The government has two policy instruments. Monetary policy consists in setting the nominal interest rate i_t. Fiscal policy consists in giving at the beginning of each period monetary transfers, denoted Γ_t in nominal terms, to the old households.[1] We will assume that the central bank redistributes all its profits, denoted as Υ_t, to the young household.[2]

An important issue, notably in the next chapter, is the specification of the information that the government can take into account when deciding on its policies in period t. We will now make this precise.

In each period the economy is hit by two stochastic shocks (α_t and Z_t). We denote by I^t the information set potentially available at date t, meaning the history of all shocks up to time t included:

$$I^t = \{(\alpha_s, Z_s) \,|\, s \leq t\} \tag{4}$$

Whenever relevant we will specify which information set the government uses to base its policy decisions. For example, in all that follows it will be assumed that fiscal policy is too slow to react to events of period t itself. Consequently fiscal policy will be function of information going up to period $t - 1$ only, which will be expressed by

$$\Gamma_t = \Gamma_t(I^{t-1}) \tag{5}$$

7.3 General Equilibrium Relations

In this and subsequent chapters we will be computing optimal policies under the three alternative assumptions of Walrasian market clearing, preset wages, and preset prices. In all three cases we need to know the equilibrium values of a number of macroeconomic variables. These general equilibrium relations are summarized in the following proposition, which we will use in all that follows.

Proposition 7.1 *In all the equilibria we will study, the following equilibrium relations hold:*

$$\Omega_{t+1} = \Omega_t + \Gamma_t \tag{6}$$

1. Note that fiscal policy is expressed differently here than in chapters 1 through 6. This is to make notation simpler in this and the next chapters; it does not change anything fundamental.

2. This assumption is made to simplify calculations; it does not change anything substantial. A similar model without this assumption is found in Bénassy (2002a).

$$P_t C_{1t} = \frac{\alpha_t(\Omega_{t+1} + \Gamma_{t+1})}{1 + i_t} \tag{7}$$

$$P_t C_{2t} = \Omega_t + \Gamma_t \tag{8}$$

If the goods market clears,

$$\frac{W_t}{P_t} = Z_t \tag{9}$$

If the labor market clears,

$$W_t = (1 + \alpha_t)(\Omega_{t+1} + \Gamma_{t+1}) \tag{10}$$

Proof Begin with the problem of the old household in period t. They start with a financial wealth Ω_t and receive a transfer Γ_t, so that they have a total amount $\Omega_t + \Gamma_t$ available. With the 100 percent cash in advance constraint (equation 2), the consumption of the old household is given by

$$P_t C_{2t} = \Omega_t + \Gamma_t \tag{11}$$

which is (8). Now we write the maximization program of the young household born in t. When young, it receives wages $W_t L_t$, profits $\Lambda_t = P_t Y_t - W_t L_t$ from the firms, and central bank profits Υ_t. It will receive Γ_{t+1} from the government when old.[3] If it consumes C_{1t} in the first period of its life, it will begin the second period with financial wealth

$$\Omega_{t+1} = (W_t L_t + \Lambda_t + \Upsilon_t) - (1 + i_t)P_t C_{1t} \tag{12}$$

In view of (11), the expected value of $\log C_{2t+1}$ is, up to an unimportant constant, equal to $\log(\Omega_{t+1} + \Gamma_{t+1})$. So the household in the first period of its life solves the following program:

$$\max \ \alpha_t \log C_{1t} + \log(\Omega_{t+1} + \Gamma_{t+1}) - (1 + \alpha_t)L_t \quad \text{s.t.}$$

$$\Omega_{t+1} = (W_t L_t + \Lambda_t + \Upsilon_t) - (1 + i_t)P_t C_{1t}$$

---

3. Note that, by assumption (5), Γ_{t+1} is function of I^t, and it is therefore known with certainty in period t.

The first-order conditions for this program yield

$$P_t C_{1t} = \frac{\alpha_t}{1 + \alpha_t} \frac{W_t L_t + \Lambda_t + \Upsilon_t + \Gamma_{t+1}}{1 + i_t} = \frac{\alpha_t}{1 + \alpha_t} \frac{P_t Y_t + \Upsilon_t + \Gamma_{t+1}}{1 + i_t} \quad (13)$$

$$L_t^s = \frac{W_t - \Lambda_t - \Upsilon_t - \Gamma_{t+1}}{W_t} \quad (14)$$

The young household borrows $P_t C_{1t}$ to satisfy its cash-in-advance constraint so that the corresponding bank profit is

$$\Upsilon_t = i_t P_t C_{1t} \quad (15)$$

The equilibrium condition on the goods market is

$$C_{1t} + C_{2t} = Y_t = Z_t L_t \quad (16)$$

Combining (11), (12), (13), (15), and (16), we obtain equations (6) to (8) which are valid in all circumstances. If the goods market clears, the real wage will be equal to the marginal productivity of labor Z_t, which yields (9). If the labor market clears, equation (14) is valid. Combined with equations (7), (8), and (15), which are always valid, we obtain (10). ∎

7.4 Optimality

7.4.1 The Criterion

To assess the optimality properties of various government policies, both in Walrasian and non-Walrasian cases, we need a criterion. Clearly, with an infinity of generations the Pareto optimality criterion is not sufficiently demanding. So we will use the criterion proposed by Samuelson for the overlapping generations model (Samuelson 1967, 1968; Abel 1987) and assume that in period t the government maximizes the following discounted sum of expected utilities V_t:

$$V_t = E_t \sum_{s=t-1}^{\infty} \beta^{s-t} U_s \quad (17)$$

In (17) the sum starts at $s = t - 1$ because the household born in $t - 1$ is still alive at time t. The limit case $\beta = 1$ corresponds to maximizing the representative household's expected utility. The parameter β plays here a role similar to that of the households' discount rate in models with infinitely lived consumers.

We can rearrange the terms in the infinite sum (17), and we find that, up to a constant, the criterion V_t can be rewritten in the more convenient form

$$V_t = E_t \sum_{s=t}^{\infty} \beta^{s-t} \Delta_s \tag{18}$$

$$\Delta_t = \alpha_t \log C_{1t} + \frac{\log C_{2t}}{\beta} - (1 + \alpha_t) L_t \tag{19}$$

7.4.2 A Characterization of Optimal States

We first want to derive the first-best allocation. The resource constraint in each period is

$$C_{1t} + C_{2t} = Z_t L_t \tag{20}$$

To find the optimal allocation, we maximize in each period the quantity Δ_t (formula 19) subject to the resource constraint (20). We obtain immediately that the first-best allocation is characterized by

$$C_{1t} = \frac{\alpha_t Z_t}{1 + \alpha_t} \tag{21}$$

$$C_{2t} = \frac{Z_t}{\beta(1 + \alpha_t)} \tag{22}$$

$$L_t = \frac{1}{1 + \alpha_t}\left(\alpha_t + \frac{1}{\beta}\right) \tag{23}$$

7.5 Optimal Policies in Walrasian Equilibrium

To contrast the Walrasian results with the cases of preset wages or prices, which we will study in the next chapter, we next compute as a benchmark optimal policies in the Walrasian case.

7.5.1 Walrasian Allocations

We can compute Walrasian allocations by combining all relations (6) through (10) found in proposition 7.1. We obtain the Walrasian wage and price as

$$W_t^* = (1 + \alpha_t)(\Omega_{t+1} + \Gamma_{t+1}) \tag{24}$$

$$P_t^* = \frac{(1 + \alpha_t)(\Omega_{t+1} + \Gamma_{t+1})}{Z_t} \tag{25}$$

and the values of consumptions and labor as

$$C_{1t} = \frac{\alpha_t Z_t}{(1 + \alpha_t)(1 + i_t)} \tag{26}$$

$$C_{2t} = \frac{(\Omega_t + \Gamma_t)Z_t}{(1 + \alpha_t)(\Omega_{t+1} + \Gamma_{t+1})} \tag{27}$$

$$L_t = \frac{\alpha_t}{(1 + \alpha_t)(1 + i_t)} + \frac{(\Omega_t + \Gamma_t)}{(1 + \alpha_t)(\Omega_{t+1} + \Gamma_{t+1})} \tag{28}$$

Note from equation (28) that if government policy is "neutral," that is, if $i_t = 0$ and $\Gamma_t = \Gamma_{t+1} = 0$ (and thus $\Omega_{t+1} = \Omega_t$), then the Walrasian quantity of labor is constant and equal to one.

7.5.2 Optimal Policies in the Walrasian Case

We are ready to characterize optimal policies when both the goods and labor markets clear:

Proposition 7.2 *Under Walrasian wages and prices the optimal monetary and fiscal policies are given by*

$$i_t = 0 \tag{29}$$

$$\frac{\Omega_t + \Gamma_t}{\Omega_t} = \beta \tag{30}$$

Proof Intuition tells us that under optimal policies the Walrasian equilibrium will be a first best. We can thus find the optimal policy by equating the first-best values of C_{1t} and C_{2t} (equations 21 and 22) and those obtained in Walrasian equilibrium (equations 26 and 27). We obtain the two conditions:

$$C_{1t} = \frac{\alpha_t Z_t}{(1 + \alpha_t)(1 + i_t)} = \frac{\alpha_t Z_t}{1 + \alpha_t} \tag{31}$$

$$C_{2t} = \frac{(\Omega_t + \Gamma_t) Z_t}{(1 + \alpha_t)(\Omega_{t+1} + \Gamma_{t+1})} = \frac{Z_t}{\beta(1 + \alpha_t)} \tag{32}$$

Simplifying equations (31) and (32), we obtain (29) and (30).   ∎

Note that formulas (29) and (30) are the two well-known "Friedman rules": set the nominal interest rate at zero, and have a monetary aggregate grow at a rate equal to the discount factor β. Both originate in Friedman's (1969) classic "optimal quantity of money" article.

In the next chapter we will focus on the issue of policy activism. A fundamental thing to note, in view of our interest in the "activism versus nonactivism" debate is that the optimal policy defined by rules (29) and (30) is a typical nonactivist policy, since the interest rate and the fiscal expansion parameter do not depend in any way on any event, past or present.

7.6   Conclusions

We constructed in this chapter a simple but rigorous model of a dynamic economy subjected to technological and demand shocks, and we derived a set of equilibrium equations applicable to situations of Walrasian equilibrium, and preset wages or prices. We then studied as a benchmark the optimal combination of fiscal and monetary policies under Walrasian market clearing, and we saw that the optimal policy is a nonactivist one, very much in line with Friedman's (1969) prescriptions. We will shortly see that this ceases to be the case when price or wage rigidities are considered, even though stringent informational conditions are imposed on policy.

7.7 References

This chapter is based on Bénassy (2002a).

The overlapping generations model has its source in Allais (1947), Samuelson (1958), and Diamond (1965).

The "Friedman rule," due to Friedman (1969), was subsequently derived by numerous authors working with infinitely lived representative agents, for example, Dornbusch and Frenkel (1973), Grandmont and Younès (1973), Brock (1975), and many others since. The Friedman rule was derived in an OLG framework by Abel (1987).

The optimality criterion is due to Samuelson (1967, 1968), and it has been developed by Abel (1987).

8

Government Information and Policy Activism

8.1 Introduction

A much debated topic in macroeconomics is whether governments should conduct activist policies and, if so, which policies. Until the early 1970s it was usually admitted, based on Keynesian intuitions, that wage or price rigidities provide a valid case for activist countercyclical demand policies. Under such rigidities unforeseen negative demand shocks generate underemployment of resources, and it was believed that government could successfully fight such underemployment by adequate demand stimulation (and conversely, for positive shocks).

This consensus disappeared at the beginning of the 1970s. Two lines of criticism arose that were particularly destructive to the Keynesian view. The first begins with Lucas's (1972) seminal work. His critique was that most models displaying policy effectiveness were not "structural," that is, not based on rigorous microfoundations. As was indeed the case, a number of results of some "nonstructural" models came from some specific ad hoc assumptions introduced into the equations of the model. So clearly effectiveness had to be investigated in the framework of a model with explicitly optimizing agents.

The second critique is due to Sargent and Wallace (1975). They showed that policy effectiveness in most traditional Keynesian models was essentially due to an "informational advantage" implicitly given to the government in such models. More precisely, the government is allowed to react to "recent" shocks while the private sector is locked into "old" wage or price contracts. Now, if the government is not allowed to use more information about shocks than the private sector, then government policies become "ineffective." This line of attack was particularly damaging, notably as most Keynesian models, even some of those constructed with rational expectations after Sargent-Wallace (1975), were vulnerable to this critique. Moreover the "informational advantage" argument is truly compelling because, even if a government has more information than the private sector, it should be considered as its duty to release any such superior information to private agents and intervene only if the result is not sufficient.

So the purpose of this chapter is to reexamine this issue in a rigorous maximizing model with preset wages or prices. In this model the economy is subject to both demand and supply shocks, and the government is "less informed" than the private sector, in the sense seen above. More precisely, we will assume that (1) the government takes its policy actions on the basis of information that is never superior to that of the private sector, and (2) the private sector sets wages or prices *after* the government has decided on policy for the same period. That is to say, the government cannot "surprise" the private sector while the latter is locked into fixed wage or price agreements.

Despite these restrictions we will show that the optimal policy is an activist one. Notably we will obtain the remarkable result that although the economy is hit in each period by stochastic demand and supply shocks *after* wages or prices have been preset, our optimal policy will nevertheless succeed in keeping the economy on a track where both labor and goods markets clear.

8.2 The Sargent-Wallace Argument

Before going in the next sections to a rigorous maximizing model, it may be useful to restate the argument in a simple model. We give here a particularly simple version of the Sargent-Wallace argument against activist policies when the government is no more informed than the private sector. Although this argument holds in more complex models, the basic idea remains the same. So for expositional simplicity we consider a highly streamlined version.

8.2.1 The Model

Consider an economy with the simple production function (everything is expressed in logarithms in this section)

$$y_t = \ell_t \tag{1}$$

The supply of labor is fixed,

$$\ell_t^s = \ell_0 \tag{2}$$

and we have a simple loglinear demand,

$$y_t = m_t + v_t - p_t \tag{3}$$

where v_t is a velocity shock. This model solves easily. The price is equal to the wage:

$$p_t = w_t \tag{4}$$

The demand for labor is thus, after combining (1), (3), and (4),

$$\ell_t = m_t + v_t - w_t \tag{5}$$

Equating this labor demand to the fixed labor supply (2) yields the Walrasian wage:

$$w_t^* = m_t + v_t - \ell_0 \tag{6}$$

Now, as we will do below, we make the traditional asssumption that the actual wage is preset at the expected value of the Walrasian wage:

$$w_t = E_{t-1} w_t^* = E_{t-1} m_t + E_{t-1} v_t - \ell_0 \tag{7}$$

Combining (5) and (7), we obtain the level of employment:

$$\ell_t - \ell_0 = m_t - E_{t-1} m_t + v_t - E_{t-1} v_t \tag{8}$$

Let us assume that the government's objective is to stabilize employment (actually the policies we will derive also stabilize inflation). We want to investigate two distinct possibilities, depending on what information the government is allowed to use.

8.2.2 Traditional Keynesian Analysis

In traditional Keynesian analysis, say of the IS-LM type, it is implicitly assumed that the government can use all information up to and within period t included:

$$m_t = m_t(I^t) \tag{9}$$

In such a case one optimal policy is of the type

$$m_t = \mu - v_t \tag{10}$$

Inserting (10) into (8), we find that employment is

$$\ell_t = \ell_0 \tag{11}$$

We see that government can completely stabilize employment. But clearly here the government has an enormous informational advantage over the private sector. The private sector is locked into wage contracts based on period $t-1$ information, whereas the government can react with full knowledge of period t shocks.

8.2.3 The Ineffectiveness Result

Let us now suppose, as Sargent-Wallace (1975) suggested, that government can only use period $t-1$ information:

$$m_t = m_t(I^{t-1}) \tag{12}$$

Then $m_t - E_{t-1}m_t$ and $v_t - E_{t-1}v_t$ in formula (8) are independant. If the government wants to reduce fluctuations in employment, the best it can do is to have a fully predictable policy such that

$$m_t = E_{t-1}m_t \tag{13}$$

Under condition (13) employment is given by (equation 8)

$$\ell_t - \ell_0 = v_t - E_{t-1}v_t \tag{14}$$

No matter which policy it uses, government will therefore be unable to suppress a minimal amount of fluctuations, driven by the innovations in velocity $v_t - E_{t-1}v_t$. This is the famous "ineffectiveness" result.

In this very simple model we may note that although it cannot stabilize employment, the government can stabilize inflation by selecting, among policies characterized by (13), a policy of the type

$$m_t = \mu - E_{t-1}v_t \tag{15}$$

We can indeed compute, combining (4), (7), and (15),

$$p_t = \mu - \ell_0 \tag{16}$$

so that inflation is always equal to zero.

8.3 The Model

We now move to a model with explicit maximization, within which the ineffectiveness issue can be rigorously studied. We will use the same monetary overlapping generations model as in the previous chapter. Let us briefly recall the main elements.

8.3.1 The Agents

Households of generation t maximize the expected value of their utility U_t, with

$$U_t = \alpha_t \log C_{1t} + \log C_{2t+1} - (1 + \alpha_t)L_t \tag{17}$$

They are submitted in each period of their life to a cash-in-advance constraint:

$$M_{1t} \geq P_t C_{1t}, \quad M_{2t+1} \geq P_{t+1}C_{2t+1} \tag{18}$$

The representative firm in period t has a production function

$$Y_t = Z_t L_t \tag{19}$$

Finally the government sets the nominal interest rate i_t, and gives fiscal transfers Γ_t in nominal terms to the old households.

8.3.2   The Timing

Because the issue raised by Sargent and Wallace (1975) about the respective information of the public and private sector is central to the debate, the timing of actions and information is important. So we will spell things out precisely.

The old households enter period t holding a quantity of financial assets Ω_t carried from the previous period. During period t, events occur in three steps:

1. Government sets its two policy variables, the interest rate i_t and the transfers Γ_t. We will assume that i_t and Γ_t are functions only of macroeconomic variables up to $t-1$ included (and therefore *not* of any variable or shock revealed in period t):

$$i_t = i_t(I^{t-1}), \quad \Gamma_t = \Gamma_t(I^{t-1}) \tag{20}$$

The old households are now endowed with a quantity of assets $\Omega_t + \Gamma_t$.

2. The wage (or price) is set by the private sector at its expected market-clearing value, without knowing the values of period t shocks α_t and Z_t.

3. The shocks become known to the private sector, and transactions are carried out accordingly.

We may note that as we indicated in the introduction to this book, the government does not have the opportunity to use policy to "surprise" the private sector while it is locked into binding nominal contracts, since the price or wage contracts are signed *after* the government has taken its policy decisions i_t and Γ_t. Also policy decisions in period t, i_t and Γ_t, are based on information up to $t-1$, so the government is no more informed than the private agents.

8.4   General Equilibrium Relations

In the discussion that follows we will derive optimal policies under the two alternative assumptions of preset wages, and preset prices. We saw in the previous chapter (proposition 7.1) a number of general equilibrium relations, and we recall them here. First some relations hold in all cases:

$$P_t C_{1t} = \frac{\alpha_t(\Omega_{t+1} + \Gamma_{t+1})}{1 + i_t} \tag{21}$$

$$P_t C_{2t} = \Omega_t + \Gamma_t \tag{22}$$

$$\Omega_{t+1} = \Omega_t + \Gamma_t \tag{23}$$

If the goods market clears, we further have

$$\frac{W_t}{P_t} = Z_t \tag{24}$$

and if the labor market clears, we have

$$W_t = (1 + \alpha_t)(\Omega_{t+1} + \Gamma_{t+1}) \tag{25}$$

8.5   Preset Wages

Let us now assume that firms and workers sign wage contracts at the beginning of period t, based on information available then (which does *not* include the values of α_t and Z_t), and that at this wage households supply the quantity of labor demanded by firms. In order not to add any further distortion, we will make the assumption, traditional since Gray (1976), that the preset wage is equal to the expected value of the Walrasian wage:[1]

$$W_t = E_{t-1} W_t^* \tag{26}$$

where the expression of W_t^* is given by formula (25):

$$W_t^* = (1 + \alpha_t)(\Omega_{t+1} + \Gamma_{t+1}) \tag{27}$$

So after combining (26) and (27), we have a preset wage equal to

$$W_t = E_{t-1}[(1 + \alpha_t)(\Omega_{t+1} + \Gamma_{t+1})] \tag{28}$$

---

1. Derivations of similar relations in a framework of imperfect competition can be found, for example, in Bénassy (2002b), Woodford (2003), and the works of many other economists.

8.5.1   Computing the Equilibrium

Under preset wages, equilibrium equations (21) to (24) hold. Combining these equations, we find that the preset wage equilibrium is characterized by the following values for employment and consumptions:

$$C_{1t} = \frac{\alpha_t(\Omega_{t+1} + \Gamma_{t+1})Z_t}{(1 + i_t)W_t} \tag{29}$$

$$C_{2t} = \frac{(\Omega_t + \Gamma_t)Z_t}{W_t} \tag{30}$$

$$L_t = \frac{\alpha_t(\Omega_{t+1} + \Gamma_{t+1})}{(1 + i_t)W_t} + \frac{\Omega_t + \Gamma_t}{W_t} \tag{31}$$

8.5.2   The Suboptimality of Nonactivist Policies

To show the suboptimality of nonactivist policies, we now study what would happen if the government followed the policies that were optimal under Walrasian market clearing. These policies were derived in the previous chapter (proposition 7.2). We recall them here:

$$i_t = 0 \tag{32}$$

$$\frac{\Omega_t + \Gamma_t}{\Omega_t} = \beta \tag{33}$$

Combining (28) and (33), we find that the preset wage W_t is equal to

$$W_t = \beta(1 + \alpha_a)(\Omega_t + \Gamma_t) \tag{34}$$

with

$$\alpha_a = E(\alpha_t) \tag{35}$$

where the subscript a means "average." Combining equations (29), (30), (31), and (34), we obtain the following values for consumptions and employment:

$$C_{1t} = \frac{\alpha_t Z_t}{1 + \alpha_a} \tag{36}$$

$$C_{2t} = \frac{Z_t}{\beta(1 + \alpha_a)} \tag{37}$$

$$L_t = \frac{1 + \beta\alpha_t}{\beta(1 + \alpha_a)} \tag{38}$$

It is easy to check that the allocation defined by equations (36) to (38) is not even a Pareto optimum. Looking now at the labor market, we see that the discrepancy between the demand and supply of labor is equal to

$$L_t - L_t^s = \frac{\alpha_t - \alpha_a}{1 + \alpha_a} \tag{39}$$

The economy will display either underemployment (when $\alpha_t < \alpha_a$) or overemployment (when $\alpha_t > \alpha_a$), both creating inefficiencies. We will now show that an activist policy enables to do much better.

8.5.3 The Optimality of Activist Policies

We will now show that under preset wages optimal policies become activist. Optimal fiscal and monetary policies are characterized through the following proposition:

Proposition 8.1 *Under preset wages the optimal monetary and fiscal policies are given by*

$$i_t = 0 \tag{40}$$

$$\frac{\Omega_t + \Gamma_t}{\Omega_t} = \frac{\beta(1 + \alpha_a)}{1 + \alpha_{t-1}} \tag{41}$$

Proof To obtain the optimal policy in a simple way, we will take a slightly roundabout route. Essentially we use the fact that the value of C_{2t} in (30) is independant of the demand shock α_t. We will proceed in two steps: (1) compute the best possible situation attainable under the constraint that C_{2t} is independant of α_t and (2) show that the policy defined by (40) and (41) leads to this best situation, so as to be indeed the optimal policy.

Let us now carry out step 1. For that we maximize the expected value of the "period t utility" Δ_t:

$$\Delta_t = \alpha_t \log C_{1t} + \frac{1}{\beta} \log C_{2t} - (1 + \alpha_t)L_t \qquad (42)$$

subject to the feasibility constraint $C_{1t} + C_{2t} = Z_t L_t$ and the condition that C_{2t} be independent of α_t. Let us first insert the feasibility constraint into (42). The maximand becomes

$$\alpha_t \log C_{1t} + \frac{1}{\beta} \log C_{2t} - (1 + \alpha_t) \frac{C_{1t} + C_{2t}}{Z_t} \qquad (43)$$

Since there is no constraint on C_{1t}, we immediately find its optimal value:

$$C_{1t} = \frac{\alpha_t Z_t}{1 + \alpha_t} \qquad (44)$$

Now, taking out constant terms, we have to maximize the expected value of

$$\frac{1}{\beta} \log C_{2t} - (1 + \alpha_t) \frac{C_{2t}}{Z_t} \qquad (45)$$

under the only constraint that C_{2t} is independent of α_t. This amounts to maximizing, for every value of the shock Z_t, the expectation of (45) with respect to α_t, namely the quantity

$$\frac{1}{\beta} \log C_{2t} - (1 + \alpha_a) \frac{C_{2t}}{Z_t} \qquad (46)$$

which yields immediately

$$C_{2t} = \frac{Z_t}{\beta(1 + \alpha_a)} \qquad (47)$$

We are ready to move to step 2. We will see that policies (40) and (41) allow us to reach the allocation defined by (44) and (47). To show this, we equalize the equilibrium values in (29) and (30) to those we just found (44 and 47):

$$C_{1t} = \frac{\alpha_t(\Omega_{t+1} + \Gamma_{t+1})Z_t}{(1+i_t)W_t} = \frac{\alpha_t Z_t}{1+\alpha_t} \tag{48}$$

$$C_{2t} = \frac{(\Omega_t + \Gamma_t)Z_t}{W_t} = \frac{Z_t}{\beta(1+\alpha_a)} \tag{49}$$

Taking first equation (48), and comparing it with the value of the Walrasian wage W_t^* (equation 27), we obtain

$$W_t = \frac{(1+\alpha_t)(\Omega_{t+1} + \Gamma_{t+1})}{1+i_t} = \frac{W_t^*}{1+i_t} \tag{50}$$

Given that $W_t = E_{t-1}W_t^*$, the only way to make these consistent is to have $i_t = 0$ (equation 40). Inserting this value $i_t = 0$ into equations (48) and (49) yields

$$\Omega_{t+1} + \Gamma_{t+1} = \frac{W_t}{1+\alpha_t} \tag{51}$$

$$W_t = \beta(1+\alpha_a)(\Omega_t + \Gamma_t) \tag{52}$$

Combining (51), (52), and $\Omega_{t+1} = \Omega_t + \Gamma_t$, we finally obtain the optimal fiscal policy (equation 41). ∎

The optimal monetary-fiscal policy consists of equations (40) and (41). The monetary rule is the same as in the Walrasian case ($i_t = 0$), but the optimal fiscal policy (41) is now an activist countercyclical one: a negative demand shock yesterday (low α_{t-1}) triggers high transfers today (high Γ_t) and conversely for a positive demand shock.

We see that rule (41) combines in a nutshell both some Friedmanian and Keynesian insights. Indeed we can observe that if there were no demand shocks, namely if α_t was constant, equation (41) would yield $\Omega_t + \Gamma_t = \beta\Omega_t$, the traditional Friedman rule, which we found to be optimal in the Walrasian case. However, we also see that as soon as demand shocks are present, the optimal policy calls for the government to respond countercyclically to these shocks, since a negative demand shock today (low α_t) will trigger higher transfers Γ_{t+1} tomorrow, and conversely for a positive demand shock. The optimal policy is thus an activist one.

Let us note that since $i_t = 0$, equation (50) can be rewritten as

$$W_t = W_t^* \tag{53}$$

So, although the wage is preset before the shocks are revealed, the labor market is always cleared under our optimal policy! Note, however, comparing (49) with equation (22) of the previous chapter, that the optimal policy of proposition 8.1 does not allow us to reach the first-best optimum. Nominal rigidities still result in some residual efficiency cost, although our optimal policy clearly attenuates this cost.

8.5.4   An Intuitive Explanation

The fact that a government with no more information than the private sector can nevertheless succeed in stabilizing the economy, despite wages being set in advance without knowledge of the shocks, may be quite surprising. So we will give here a simple intuition behind this remarkable result. Let us set the interest rate at zero, and rewrite the young household's consumption function (equation 13 in the previous chapter) as

$$P_t C_{1t} = \frac{\alpha_t}{1 + \alpha_t} (P_t Y_t + \Gamma_{t+1}) \tag{54}$$

Suppose that after the wage has been set, a negative demand shock (a low α_t) hits the economy. If the government has no systematic policy, this shock will clearly lead, in view of this consumption function, to a *decrease* in the demand for goods and labor, and to underemployment of labor. Now, if the government is known to conduct the countercyclical policy (41), then the private sector will know in advance that the future transfers Γ_{t+1} will be high. So, by the formula above this will, on the contrary, tend to *increase* the demand for goods and labor. When policy is calibrated to be (41), these two conflicting effects cancel out, and the economy remains at full employment. Of course, the zero unemployment result is due to our particular specifications, but the fact that an adequate activist policy can be beneficial is a robust result.

8.5.5 Implementation

Policy (41) is expressed as a function of shocks α_t. But these shocks, which are shocks to the households' utility functions, may not be directly observable by the government. So we will now check whether such policy can actually be implemented, namely whether the value of α_t can be recouped from observable macroeconomic series. We will see that this is feasible.

Let us indeed insert the value of the optimal policy (41) into the values of the wage and employment in a preset wage equilibrium (equations 28 and 31). We obtain

$$W_t = \beta(1 + \alpha_a)(\Omega_t + \Gamma_t) \tag{55}$$

$$L_t = \left[\frac{\beta(1 + \alpha_a)\alpha_t}{1 + \alpha_t} + 1\right]\frac{\Omega_t + \Gamma_t}{W_t} \tag{56}$$

Combining these two equations, we find the value of employment as a function of the current shock:

$$L_t = \frac{\alpha_t}{1 + \alpha_t} + \frac{1}{\beta(1 + \alpha_a)} \tag{57}$$

If this relation is inverted, the shock α_t can be deduced from the value of employment:

$$\frac{1}{1 + \alpha_t} = 1 - L_t + \frac{1}{\beta(1 + \alpha_a)} \tag{58}$$

With (58) inserted into (41), the policy rule (41) can be rewritten directly as a function of observable employment:

$$\frac{\Omega_t + \Gamma_t}{\Omega_t} = 1 + \beta(1 + \alpha_a) - \beta(1 + \alpha_a)L_{t-1} \tag{59}$$

Under this form we see clearly that the optimal policy can be implemented, since the policy rule is now directly function of observable macroeconomic variables, more precisely the past value of employment.

8.6   Preset Prices

So far we have concentrated on nominal wage rigidities. In order to be complete, we should also investigate price rigidities. So we will now assume that instead of wages, it is prices that are preset according to the formula

$$P_t = E_{t-1}P_t^*$$ (60)

The Walrasian price P_t^* was computed in the preceding chapter as

$$P_t^* = \frac{(1 + \alpha_t)(\Omega_{t+1} + \Gamma_{t+1})}{Z_t}$$ (61)

So, combining (60) and (61), we find that the preset price is equal to

$$P_t = E_{t-1}\left[\frac{(1 + \alpha_t)(\Omega_{t+1} + \Gamma_{t+1})}{Z_t}\right]$$ (62)

8.6.1   Computing the Equilibrium

Equation (24), representing the firms' goods supply behavior, no longer holds because the price is preset. The other equilibrium equations (21), (22), (23), and (25) are valid. Combining them, we obtain the values of the preset price equilibrium quantities:

$$C_{1t} = \frac{\alpha_t(\Omega_{t+1} + \Gamma_{t+1})}{(1 + i_t)P_t}$$ (63)

$$C_{2t} = \frac{\Omega_t + \Gamma_t}{P_t}$$ (64)

$$L_t = \frac{\alpha_t(\Omega_{t+1} + \Gamma_{t+1})}{(1 + i_t)P_tZ_t} + \frac{\Omega_t + \Gamma_t}{P_tZ_t}$$ (65)

8.6.2   Optimal Policies

We now characterize the optimal fiscal and monetary policies by the following proposition:

Proposition 8.2 *Under preset prices the optimal monetary and fiscal policies are given by*

$$i_t = 0 \tag{66}$$

$$\frac{\Omega_t + \Gamma_t}{\Omega_t} = \frac{\beta(1 + \alpha_a)Z_{t-1}}{(1 + \alpha_{t-1})Z_a} \tag{67}$$

where

$$\alpha_a = E(\alpha_t), \quad \frac{1}{Z_a} = E\left(\frac{1}{Z_t}\right) \tag{68}$$

Proof Following the method of section 8.5 above, we note that the value of C_{2t} in (64) is independant of both the demand shock α_t and the productivity shock Z_t. We thus maximize again the expected value of Δ_t:

$$\Delta_t = \alpha_t \log C_{1t} + \frac{1}{\beta} \log C_{2t} - (1 + \alpha_t)L_t \tag{69}$$

subject to the feasibility constraint $C_{1t} + C_{2t} = Z_t L_t$ and, this time, to the condition that C_{2t} be independent of both α_t and Z_t. We obtain

$$C_{1t} = \frac{\alpha_t Z_t}{1 + \alpha_t}, \quad C_{2t} = \frac{Z_a}{\beta(1 + \alpha_a)} \tag{70}$$

Now, if a set of government policies allows to reach these values, it will be the optimal one. We thus equalize the values in (63) and (64) to those we just found (70):

$$C_{1t} = \frac{\alpha_t(\Omega_{t+1} + \Gamma_{t+1})}{(1 + i_t)P_t} = \frac{\alpha_t Z_t}{1 + \alpha_t} \tag{71}$$

$$C_{2t} = \frac{\Omega_t + \Gamma_t}{P_t} = \frac{Z_a}{\beta(1 + \alpha_a)} \tag{72}$$

Using first equation (71), and comparing it with the value of the Walrasian price P_t^* (equation 61), we obtain

$$P_t = \frac{(1 + \alpha_t)(\Omega_{t+1} + \Gamma_{t+1})}{(1 + i_t)Z_t} = \frac{P_t^*}{1 + i_t} \tag{73}$$

Since $P_t = E_{t-1}P_t^*$, the only way to make these consistent is to have $i_t = 0$ (equation 66). Inserting $i_t = 0$ into equations (71) and (72) results in

$$\Omega_{t+1} + \Gamma_{t+1} = \frac{P_t Z_t}{1 + \alpha_t} \tag{74}$$

$$P_t = \frac{\beta(1 + \alpha_a)(\Omega_t + \Gamma_t)}{Z_a} \tag{75}$$

Combining (74) and (75), and lagging one period, we obtain the optimal fiscal policy (equation 67). ∎

The interest rate rule is again the same as in the Walrasian situation ($i_t = 0$). The optimal fiscal policy (67), as in the preset wages case, reacts countercyclically to demand shocks α_t. Moreover it now reacts positively to productivity shocks Z_t. This might appear like an element of procyclical policy, but actually it does not if we look at things from the point of view of the labor market: under rigid prices, a positive productivity shock creates a *negative* shock on labor market demand. It is thus natural in such a case to want to engineer a demand expansion so as to bring labor market balance, and this policy is countercyclical from the point of view of the labor market.

Our policy has further the same remarkable feature as in the preset wage case. Indeed, with $i_t = 0$, equation (73) becomes

$$P_t = P_t^* \tag{76}$$

So, although the price is preset before the shocks are revealed, the goods market is always cleared under our optimal policy. The basic intuition is very similar to that which we gave for the preset wages case (section 8.5.4).

8.6.3   Implementation

Again, we want to know whether policy (67) can be expressed in terms of observable variables. The technology shock Z_t is observable, since it is equal to Y_t/L_t. For the demand shock we combine (19), (65), (66), (67), and (75) to obtain

$$\frac{1}{1+\alpha_t} = 1 - \frac{\beta(1+\alpha_a)Y_t - Z_a}{\beta(1+\alpha_a)Z_t} \tag{77}$$

Inserting this into (67), we obtain the optimal fiscal policy rule:

$$\frac{\Omega_t + \Gamma_t}{\Omega_t} = 1 + \beta(1+\alpha_a)\frac{Z_{t-1}}{Z_a} - \beta(1+\alpha_a)\frac{Y_{t-1}}{Z_a} \tag{78}$$

We already saw that a positive technology shock will lead to higher transfers. As for output, for a given technology shock low output signals a low demand shock, which calls for an expansive countercyclical policy, hence the negative sign on Y_{t-1}.

8.7 Conclusions

We constructed in this chapter a simple but rigorous model of a dynamic economy submitted to technological and demand shocks, and studied the optimal combination of fiscal and monetary policies under the two regimes of preset wages and preset prices.

An important question that motivated this investigation was whether these policies should be activist, that is, whether government should respond to observed shocks. An important issue within this debate is that uncovered by Sargent and Wallace (1975), namely should policy be activist even when government has no more information than the public sector?

We saw in the previous chapter that if prices and wages are Walrasian, then the optimal monetary policy is to have the nominal interest rate set to zero, and the optimal fiscal policy is to have the stock of financial assets grow at the rate β, where β is the discount rate. These are the two "Friedman rules" (Friedman 1969), and these policies are nonactivist.

Now, if wages are preset, the optimal monetary policy is still to maintain the nominal interest rate at zero, but the optimal fiscal policy becomes activist and countercyclical, in the sense that the fiscal transfers are negatively related to past demand shocks.

If prices are preset, the optimal monetary policy remains the same. Fiscal policy reacts negatively to demand shocks, and now positively to technology shocks.

Our results are not subject to the usual critiques against activist policies, since (1) the model is microfounded and (2) the government is always "less informed" than the private sector, and this issue of government information was the central objection of Sargent and Wallace (1975) to activist policies. With our specification of the model the government can even maintain the economy at all times on a full-employment trajectory.

However, not any combination of shocks and rigidities is conducive to policy activism. So we will qualify our results some more.

First, we note that there is a clear-cut difference between the prescriptions for fiscal and monetary policy: the optimal monetary policy is always to maintain the nominal interest rate at zero so that this part of the policy remains nonactivist. On the other hand, the optimal fiscal policy will respond in a countercyclical manner to demand shocks α_t, whether wages or prices are rigid.

Second, the optimal reaction to a particular shock depends very much on the underlying rigidity. We saw, for example, that in this model, fiscal policy should not react to technology shocks if wages are rigid but should react positively if prices are rigid.

So, while activist policies are superior to nonactivist ones, it is clear that a detailed knowledge of the economy's rigidities and shocks is necessary before a government can embark on such policies.

8.8   References

This chapter is based on Bénassy (2001, 2002a).

The "ineffectiveness" argument according to which a government no more informed than the private sector could be powerless against employment fluctuations was developed by Sargent and Wallace (1975).

Subsequently the important idea that a "less informed government" can nevertheless have stabilizing powers was developed in insightful articles by Turnovsky (1980), Weiss (1980), King (1982, 1983), and Andersen (1986). All of these papers embed a sophisticated treatment of rational expectations into an otherwise fairly traditional framework, with a priori given demand-supply functions and government objectives. So the question of whether these results can carry over to a model with explicit maximization had remained open.

9

Fiscal Policy and Optimal Interest Rate Rules

9.1 Introduction

In the previous chapter we saw that the optimal policies in an economy with wage or price rigidities are activist, even under stringent informational constraints. On the other hand, we also saw that although the optimal fiscal policy is an activist one, the monetary policy is not, respecting the Friedman rule $i_t = 0$ at all times. This is in clear contrast to the literature on interest rate rules, where the interest rate is notably supposed to react to the rate of inflation.

One thing we may note, however, is that in chapter 8 we assumed that the "delay of reaction" was exactly the same for fiscal and monetary policy, namely both policies in period t reacted to shocks up to period $t - 1$. But most people agree that in reality, and in view of the various actual institutional constraints, fiscal policy reacts much more slowly than monetary policy.

So in this chapter we will go to the other extreme, and assume that monetary policy can react immediately, whereas fiscal policy cannot react sufficiently fast to be of any positive utility. We will find that in such circumstances optimal monetary policy will become activist, very much in step with what is described in the literature on interest rate rules.

Optimal rules will be naturally expressed as functions of shocks. We will further note that when we express the optimal policy as a function of observable endogenous variables, inflation does not necessarily emerge as the best argument. For example, we will see optimal rules where the most natural arguments are employment or output.

9.2   The Model

As in the two previous chapters we consider a monetary overlapping generations model with production. Households of generation t maximize the expected value of their utility U_t, with

$$U_t = \alpha_t \log C_{1t} + \log C_{2t+1} - (1 + \alpha_t)L_t \qquad (1)$$

where α_t is a positive stochastic variable. Households are submitted in each period of their life to a cash-in-advance constraint:

$$M_{1t} \geq P_t C_{1t}, \quad M_{2t+1} \geq P_{t+1} C_{2t+1} \qquad (2)$$

The representative firm has a production function

$$Y_t = Z_t L_t \qquad (3)$$

We assume that the stochastic shocks α_t and Z_t are independent i.i.d. variables.

9.2.1   Government Policy

Government policy potentially includes both monetary policy, which consists in setting the interest rate i_t, and fiscal policy, which consists in setting the fiscal transfer Γ_t.

In order to clearly differentiate the exercises carried out in this and the previous chapter, let us make explicit some informational assumptions. As in the previous chapters we denote by I^t the history of the shocks up to time t included.

In the previous chapter, in order to respect the informational requirements initiated by Sargent and Wallace (1975), we assumed that both policy variables were function of information up to period $t - 1$ only:

$$i_t = i_t(I^{t-1}), \quad \Gamma_t = \Gamma_t(I^{t-1}), \qquad \forall t \qquad (4)$$

As we indicated in the introduction, we will assume in this chapter that fiscal transfers are not used actively, and to simplify the exposition, we will simply assume that they are zero at all times. On the other hand, we also assume, following the recent literature on interest rate rules, that the central bank is allowed to react to the *current* shocks in addition to past shocks. So in this chapter government policies will be characterized by

$$i_t = i_t(I^t), \quad \Gamma_t = 0, \qquad \forall t \qquad (5)$$

We may note that it is not clear a priori which policy package, (4) or (5), will perform best, since (4) has two policy instruments but (5) uses more recent information.

9.2.2 The Optimality Criterion

As in the two previous chapters the government chooses its optimal policy so as to maximize

$$V_t = E_t \sum_{s=t}^{\infty} \beta^{s-t} \Delta_s \qquad (6)$$

with

$$\Delta_t = \alpha_t \log C_{1t} + \frac{\log C_{2t}}{\beta} - (1 + \alpha_t) L_t \qquad (7)$$

9.3 General Equilibrium Relations

For the policy evaluations that follow, we will again need to know the equilibrium values of a number of macroeconomic variables.

Proposition 9.1 *In the equilibria we consider the following equilibrium relations to hold:*

$$P_t C_{1t} = \frac{\alpha_t \Omega_t}{1 + i_t} \qquad (8)$$

$$P_t C_{2t} = \Omega_t \tag{9}$$

If the goods market clears, we further have

$$\frac{W_t}{P_t} = Z_t \tag{10}$$

If the labor market clears, we have

$$W_t = (1 + \alpha_t)\Omega_t \tag{11}$$

Proof Use proposition 7.1 in chapter 7 with $\Gamma_t = \Gamma_{t+1} = 0$. ∎

9.4   Optimal Interest Policy: The Walrasian Case

As a benchmark, we now compute the optimal interest rate policy in the case where all markets clear. From equations (10) and (11) we find the Walrasian wage and price:

$$W_t^* = (1 + \alpha_t)\Omega_t \tag{12}$$

$$P_t^* = \frac{(1 + \alpha_t)\Omega_t}{Z_t} \tag{13}$$

Proposition 9.2   *Under Walrasian prices and wages the optimal interest rate rule is*

$$i_t = 0 \tag{14}$$

Proof The central bank must choose the interest rate so as to maximize, in each period and for each value of the shocks,

$$\Delta_t = \alpha_t \log C_{1t} + \frac{1}{\beta} \log C_{2t} - (1 + \alpha_t)L_t \tag{15}$$

or, since $C_{1t} + C_{2t} = Z_t L_t$,

$$\Delta_t = \alpha_t \log C_{1t} + \frac{1}{\beta} \log C_{2t} - \frac{C_{1t} + C_{2t}}{Z_t} \tag{16}$$

We first note that C_{2t} (equation 9) does not depend on the interest rate, since P_t^* does not (equation 13). Combining (8) and (13), we find that C_{1t} is given by

$$C_{1t} = \frac{\alpha_t Z_t}{(1 + \alpha_t)(1 + i_t)} \tag{17}$$

This value of C_{1t} is inserted into (16). Then maximizing Δ_t with respect to i_t yields immediately (14). ∎

We see that in the Walrasian case, no matter what are the shocks, the interest rate should remain equal to zero at all times. This is again the "Friedman rule" (Friedman 1969).

9.5 Preset Wages

We begin our study of nominal rigidities with preset wages. We assume again that the preset wage is equal to the expected value of the Walrasian wage:

$$W_t = E_{t-1} W_t^* \tag{18}$$

The value of W_t^* is given in equation (12), so the preset wage is equal to

$$W_t = E_{t-1}[(1 + \alpha_t)\Omega_t] \tag{19}$$

9.5.1 The Preset Wage Equilibrium

At the preset wage equilibrium equations (8), (9), and (10) hold. So the various quantities are given by the following relations:

$$C_{1t} = \frac{\alpha_t \Omega_t Z_t}{(1 + i_t) W_t} \tag{20}$$

$$C_{2t} = \frac{\Omega_t Z_t}{W_t} \tag{21}$$

$$L_t = \frac{\alpha_t \Omega_t}{(1 + i_t) W_t} + \frac{\Omega_t}{W_t} \tag{22}$$

9.5.2 The Optimal Interest Rate Rule

We now compute the optimal interest rate as a function of the shocks.

Proposition 9.3 *Under preset wages the optimal interest rate rule is*

$$i_t = \max\left(0, \frac{1+\alpha_t}{1+\alpha_a} - 1\right) \qquad (23)$$

with

$$\alpha_a = E(\alpha_t) \qquad (24)$$

Proof From (19) we first find the value of the wage:

$$W_t = E_{t-1}[(1+\alpha_t)\Omega_t] = (1+\alpha_a)\Omega_t \qquad (25)$$

Inserting (25) into formulas (20), (21), and (22), we find the values of C_{1t}, C_{2t}, and L_t at the preset wage equilibrium:

$$C_{1t} = \frac{\alpha_t Z_t}{(1+i_t)(1+\alpha_a)} \qquad (26)$$

$$C_{2t} = \frac{Z_t}{1+\alpha_a} \qquad (27)$$

$$L_t = \frac{\alpha_t}{(1+i_t)(1+\alpha_a)} + \frac{1}{1+\alpha_a} \qquad (28)$$

Now we insert these values of consumptions and labor into the criterion Δ_t (equation 7). So the government has to maximize with respect to i_t and for each value of the shocks,

$$\alpha_t \log\left[\frac{\alpha_t Z_t}{(1+i_t)(1+\alpha_a)}\right] + \frac{1}{\beta}\log\left(\frac{Z_t}{1+\alpha_a}\right) - \frac{(1+\alpha_t)}{(1+\alpha_a)}\left(\frac{\alpha_t}{1+i_t}+1\right) \qquad (29)$$

subject to the constraint $i_t \geq 0$. The solution is rule (23). ∎

The optimal interest rate rule is function of the demand shock α_t. We note that this optimal interest rate rule is nonlinear: it dampens the effects of the demand shock when it is above average, namely when $\alpha_t > \alpha_a$. But it is totally inactive for deflationary shocks because of the constraint $i_t \geq 0$.

We may also inquire how well the labor market is stabilized through this rule. Here a good indicator is the discrepancy between labor demand and labor supply, which can be computed as

$$L_t - L_t^s = \frac{\alpha_t - \alpha_a}{1 + \alpha_a} \qquad (30)$$

We see that the interest rate policy is powerless to cure employment imbalances.

9.5.3 A Comparison of Policies

We may want to compare the performances of the interest rule of this chapter, and of the policy package studied in the previous chapter.

As far as the labor market is concerned, the performances of the two policies are somewhat unequal. The combination of optimal fiscal and monetary policies of the previous chapter completely eliminates imbalances in the labor market, even though it uses information from previous periods only.

As we just saw in the previous section, the optimal interest rate rule cannot prevent shocks from creating labor market imbalances, even if it makes full use of all current information.

9.5.4 Implementation

We will now express the optimal interest rule as a function of observable variables. Traditionally in this literature inflation is the principal instrument. We will see that the level of employment emerges as a natural argument of the policy rule, and can be used as a perfect surrogate for the arguments of the interest rate rule in proposition 9.3.

Proposition 9.4 *Under preset wages, if employment L_t is used as an instrument, the optimal interest rate rule is*

$$\frac{i_t}{1 + i_t} = \max[0, (1 + \alpha_a)(L_t - 1)] \qquad (31)$$

Rule (31) allows to reach the same level of utility as rule (23).

Proof If the optimal policy (23) is used, we can compute, combining (23) and (28), the level of employment:

$$L_t = \min\left(\frac{\alpha_t}{1+\alpha_t} + \frac{1}{1+\alpha_a}, \frac{\alpha_t}{1+\alpha_a} + \frac{1}{1+\alpha_a}\right) \tag{32}$$

Inverting this relation, we can deduce from L_t the value of the demand shock α_t:

$$\frac{1}{1+\alpha_t} = \min\left[1 - L_t + \frac{1}{1+\alpha_a}, \frac{1}{(1+\alpha_a)L_t}\right] \tag{33}$$

Now the optimal rule (23) can be rewritten as

$$\frac{1}{1+i_t} = \min\left(1, \frac{1+\alpha_a}{1+\alpha_t}\right) \tag{34}$$

We insert the value of $1/(1+\alpha_t)$ given by (33) into the optimal rule (34), which yields

$$\frac{1}{1+i_t} = \min\left[1, (1+\alpha_a)(1-L_t) + 1, \frac{1}{L_t}\right] \tag{35}$$

It is easy to check that the third term is always larger than the minimum of the two first ones, so we can suppress it. Subtracting from 1, we obtain the optimal rule (31). Furthermore there is a one to one relation between L_t and α_t (equation 32), and rule (31) allows to reach the same utility as the optimal rule in proposition 9.3. ∎

9.6   Preset Prices

We will now assume that instead of wages it is the prices that are preset according to the formula

$$P_t = E_{t-1}P_t^* \tag{36}$$

Combining (13) and (36), we find that the preset price is equal to

$$P_t = E_{t-1}\left[\frac{(1+\alpha_t)\Omega_t}{Z_t}\right] \tag{37}$$

9.6.1 The Preset Price Equilibrium

Under preset prices equations (3), (8), and (9) hold. Combining them yields the values of the preset price equilibrium quantities:

$$C_{1t} = \frac{\alpha_t \Omega_t}{(1 + i_t) P_t} \tag{38}$$

$$C_{2t} = \frac{\Omega_t}{P_t} \tag{39}$$

$$L_t = \frac{\alpha_t \Omega_t}{(1 + i_t) P_t Z_t} + \frac{\Omega_t}{P_t Z_t} \tag{40}$$

9.6.2 Optimal Policy

We will study the optimal interest rate rule, assuming that the monetary authority sets interest rates under full knowledge of all shocks.

Proposition 9.5 *Under preset prices the optimal interest rate rule is*

$$i_t = \max\left[0, \frac{(1 + \alpha_t) Z_a}{(1 + \alpha_a) Z_t} - 1\right] \tag{41}$$

where

$$\alpha_a = E(\alpha_t), \quad \frac{1}{Z_a} = E\left(\frac{1}{Z_t}\right) \tag{42}$$

Proof From (37) the preset price is equal to

$$P_t = E_{t-1}\left[\frac{(1 + \alpha_t)\Omega_t}{Z_t}\right] = \frac{(1 + \alpha_a)\Omega_t}{Z_a} \tag{43}$$

Combining (38), (39), (40), and (43), we obtain the equilibrium quantities

$$C_{1t} = \frac{\alpha_t \Omega_t}{(1 + i_t) P_t} = \frac{\alpha_t Z_a}{(1 + i_t)(1 + \alpha_a)} \tag{44}$$

$$C_{2t} = \frac{\Omega_t}{P_t} = \frac{Z_a}{1 + \alpha_a} \qquad (45)$$

$$L_t = \frac{Z_a}{(1 + \alpha_a)Z_t}\left(\frac{\alpha_t}{1 + i_t} + 1\right) \qquad (46)$$

We insert the values (44), (45), and (46) into the maximand Δ_t (equation 7). So we have to maximize in i_t, for each value of the shocks:

$$\Delta_t = \alpha_t \log\left[\frac{\alpha_t Z_a}{(1 + \alpha_a)(1 + i_t)}\right] + \frac{1}{\beta}\log\left(\frac{Z_a}{1 + \alpha_a}\right)$$

$$-\frac{(1 + \alpha_t)Z_a}{(1 + \alpha_a)Z_t}\left(\frac{\alpha_t}{1 + i_t} + 1\right) \qquad (47)$$

subject to the constraint $i_t \geq 0$. The solution is formula (41). ∎

To discuss the results above, let us define the "composite shock" φ_t:

$$\varphi_t = \frac{1 + \alpha_t}{Z_t} \qquad \varphi_a = \frac{1 + \alpha_a}{Z_a} \qquad (48)$$

Rule (41) can be rewritten as

$$i_t = \max\left[0, \frac{\varphi_t}{\varphi_a} - 1\right] \qquad (49)$$

We may first note that as in the preset wages case, the optimal interest rule (41) is nonlinear in its arguments. It dampens the effects of the composite shock φ_t when it is above average, namely when $\varphi_t > \varphi_a$. But it is totally inactive for low values of this shock because of the constraint $i_t \geq 0$.

We may further inquire how much this policy stabilizes imbalances on the goods market. These imbalances are well represented by the deviations from unity of the ratio $W_t/P_t Z_t$, which is the ratio of marginal cost to price. We have already computed the value of P_t (equation 43). Now from equation (11), since the labor market clears in this case, we have

$$W_t = (1 + \alpha_t)\Omega_t \qquad (50)$$

so that

$$\frac{W_t}{P_t Z_t} = \frac{(1 + \alpha_t)Z_a}{(1 + \alpha_a)Z_t} = \frac{\varphi_t}{\varphi_a} \tag{51}$$

We see that the interest rate policy is powerless against imbalances on the goods markets, whether they are provoked by demand or productivity shocks.

We may note also, looking at formula (51), that for some values of the shocks we could have $W_t/P_t Z_t > 1$. In such a case firms would shut down rather than serve demand, as we have assumed so far. We show in the appendix that introducing imperfect competition allows us to reconcile profit maximization with the assumption that demand is always served provided that shocks are not too big.

9.6.3 A Comparison of Policies

We may also want to compare the performances of the interest rule of this chapter with those of the policy package studied in the previous chapter (proposition 8.2). As far as the goods market is concerned, the performances of the two policies are somewhat unequal. The combination of optimal fiscal and monetary policies seen in the previous chapter completely eliminates imbalances in the goods market, even if it uses information only from previous periods. Under a passive fiscal policy, the optimal monetary rule cannot prevent shocks to create goods market imbalances, even if it makes full use of all current information.

9.6.4 Implementation

We finally want to find out whether we can express the optimal interest rate rule (41) as a function of observable economic variables. The technology shock Z_t is directly observable as Y_t/L_t. We will see that we can express the optimal interest rate rule (41) as a function of Z_t and output Y_t.

Proposition 9.6 *Under preset prices, if Y_t and Z_t are used as instruments, the optimal interest rate rule is*

$$\frac{i_t}{1 + i_t} = \max\left(0, \frac{1 + \alpha_a}{Z_a}Y_t - \frac{1 + \alpha_a}{Z_a}Z_t\right) \tag{52}$$

Rule (52) allows to reach the same level of utility as rule (41).

Proof If the optimal rule (41) is used, we can compute the level of output Y_t by inserting (41) into (40), and using $Y_t = Z_t L_t$:

$$Y_t = \min\left(\frac{\alpha_t Z_t}{1 + \alpha_t} + \frac{Z_a}{1 + \alpha_a}, \frac{\alpha_t Z_a}{1 + \alpha_a} + \frac{Z_a}{1 + \alpha_a}\right) \tag{53}$$

Inverting (53), we can derive the value of the demand shock α_t from Y_t and Z_t:

$$\frac{1}{1 + \alpha_t} = \min\left[1 - \frac{Y_t}{Z_t} + \frac{Z_a}{(1 + \alpha_a)Z_t}, \frac{Z_a}{(1 + \alpha_a)Y_t}\right] \tag{54}$$

Let us rewrite the optimal rule (41) as

$$\frac{1}{1 + i_t} = \min\left[1, \frac{(1 + \alpha_a)Z_t}{(1 + \alpha_t)Z_a}\right] \tag{55}$$

Inserting (54) into (55), we obtain the optimal rule:

$$\frac{1}{1 + i_t} = \min\left[1, \frac{1 + \alpha_a}{Z_a}(Z_t - Y_t) + 1, \frac{Z_t}{Y_t}\right] \tag{56}$$

It is easy to check, using the fact that $Y_t > Z_a/(1 + \alpha_a)$ (equation 53), that the third term is always larger than the minimum of the two first ones, so that it can be suppressed. Subtracting from 1, we obtain

$$\frac{i_t}{1 + i_t} = \max\left[0, \frac{1 + \alpha_a}{Z_a}(Y_t - Z_t)\right] \tag{57}$$

which is the optimal rule (52). Again, because knowledge of Y_t and Z_t allows to recoup exactly the value of α_t (equation 54), rule (52) allows us to reach the same utility as the optimal rule (41) in proposition 9.5.   ∎

The reasons why the interest rate reacts negatively to Z_t and positively to Y_t are similar to those we used to explain the optimal fiscal policy in the previous chapter: under preset prices a large value of Z_t creates a negative shock on employment, so it is natural to lower interest rates in such a situation. Then, for given Z_t, a high Y_t signals a positive demand shock, which calls for an increase in the interest rate.

9.7   Conclusions

We saw in this chapter that the passiveness of monetary policy disappears as soon as we put constraints on the fiscal transfers, and that we obtain active interest rate rules similar to those in the corresponding literature. This activity of monetary policy appears thus, at least partly, as a surrogate for that of fiscal policy.

We also found that in some circumstances it is adequate for interest rate rules to react to employment or output, whereas inflation is the argument most generally favored in the literature.

9.8   References

This chapter is based on Bénassy (2003c).

The study of interest rate rules has gained popularity since the stimulating article by Taylor (1993). Surveys and original contributions on optimal rules are found, among others, in Clarida, Gali, and Gertler (1999), Erceg, Henderson, and Levin (2000), McCallum (1999), Taylor (1999), and Woodford (2003).

A related line of literature has studied the joint determination of monetary and fiscal policies in a rigorous intertemporal framework, quite often including distortionary taxes. See, for example, Lucas and Stokey (1983) and Chari, Christiano, and Kehoe (1991).

Appendix: Imperfect Competition and Demand Satisfaction

We saw in deriving the optimal monetary rule in the preset prices case (section 9.6) that for some values of the shocks firms would make negative profits by serving demand, and therefore that they would rather shut down in the corresponding states of the world.

In this appendix we introduce imperfect competition à la Dixit-Stiglitz (1977). We show that provided that shocks are not too big (in a way that will be made precise below in formula 76), firms will always be willing to satisfy the demand for goods.

The Model

Consider the preset prices case. The households are exactly the same. Production is now carried out in two steps. Monopolistically competitive intermediate firms indexed by $j \in [0, 1]$ produce intermediate goods j with labor according to the production functions:

$$Y_{jt} = Z_t L_{jt} \tag{58}$$

where Z_t is a common productivity shock. These intermediate goods are assembled by competitive firms endowed with the technology

$$Y_t = \left(\int_0^1 Y_{jt}^\sigma \right)^{1/\sigma}, \qquad 0 < \sigma < 1 \tag{59}$$

We further assume that each firm j has its production subsidized at a rate $1/\sigma$, so that the profits of firm j are equal to

$$\Lambda_{jt} = \frac{1}{\sigma} P_{jt} Y_{jt} - W_t L_{jt} \tag{60}$$

Such subsidies are traditionally introduced in order to counteract some negative welfare effects of imperfect competition. The subsidy rate is equal to the "monopolistic markup" $1/\sigma$ associated with the function (59).

Price Setting

The final output firms maximize profits subject to the production function:

$$\text{Maximize } P_t Y_t - \sum_j P_{jt} Y_{jt} \quad \text{s.t.}$$

$$Y_t = \left(\int_0^1 Y_{jt}^\sigma \right)^{1/\sigma}, \qquad 0 < \sigma < 1$$

This yields the demand for intermediate good j:

$$Y_{jt} = Y_t \left(\frac{P_{jt}}{P_t} \right)^{-1/(1-\sigma)} \tag{61}$$

where P_t is the usual CES aggregator

$$P_t = \left(\int_0^1 P_{jt}^{-\sigma/(1-\sigma)} \, dj \right)^{-(1-\sigma)/\sigma} \tag{62}$$

Accordingly the profits of firm j are equal to

$$\Lambda_{jt} = \frac{1}{\sigma} P_t Y_t \left(\frac{P_{jt}}{P_t} \right)^{-\sigma/(1-\sigma)} - \frac{W_t Y_t}{Z_t} \left(\frac{P_{jt}}{P_t} \right)^{-1/(1-\sigma)} \tag{63}$$

Maximization in P_{jt} yields the following first-order condition:

$$P_{jt} = P_t^m = \frac{W_t}{Z_t} \tag{64}$$

Now we will assume that the preset price P_t (which is the same for all firms) is equal to the expected value of this "monopolistically competitive price" P_t^m. This yields, using (11),

$$P_t = E_{t-1} P_t^m = E_{t-1} \left(\frac{W_t}{Z_t} \right) = E_{t-1} \left[\frac{(1+\alpha_t)\Omega_t}{Z_t} \right] \tag{65}$$

The Optimal Interest Rate Rule

Again, we assume that the monetary authority sets interest rates under full knowledge of all shocks.

Proposition 9.7 *The optimal interest rate rule under preset prices is*

$$i_t = \max \left[0, \frac{(1+\alpha_t)Z_a}{(1+\alpha_a)Z_t} - 1 \right] = \max \left[0, \frac{\varphi_t}{\varphi_a} - 1 \right] \tag{66}$$

Proof From (65) we find that the preset price is equal to

$$P_t = E_{t-1} \left[\frac{(1+\alpha_t)\Omega_t}{Z_t} \right] = \frac{(1+\alpha_a)\Omega_t}{Z_a} \tag{67}$$

The associated equilibrium quantities are

$$C_{1t} = \frac{\alpha_t \Omega_t}{(1 + i_t)P_t} = \frac{\alpha_t Z_a}{(1 + i_t)(1 + \alpha_a)} \tag{68}$$

$$C_{2t} = \frac{\Omega_t}{P_t} = \frac{Z_a}{1 + \alpha_a} \tag{69}$$

$$L_t = \frac{Z_a}{(1 + \alpha_a)Z_t}\left(\frac{\alpha_t}{1 + i_t} + 1\right) \tag{70}$$

Let us insert (68), (69), and (70) into Δ_t (formula 7). We have to maximize in i_t for each value of the shocks:

$$\Delta_t = \alpha_t \log\left[\frac{\alpha_t Z_a}{(1 + \alpha_a)(1 + i_t)}\right] + \frac{1}{\beta}\log\left(\frac{Z_a}{1 + \alpha_a}\right)$$

$$- \frac{(1 + \alpha_t)Z_a}{(1 + \alpha_a)Z_t}\left(\frac{\alpha_t}{1 + i_t} + 1\right) \tag{71}$$

subject to the constraint $i_t \geq 0$. The solution is formula (66).   ∎

Note that the interest rate rule is the same as that which we found in proposition 9.5. Next we compute in which circumstances firms will be actually willing to serve all demand forthcoming to them. Taking into account the subsidy, we write the profit of a firm j (formulas 58 and 60) as

$$\Lambda_{jt} = \frac{1}{\sigma}P_t Y_{jt} - W_t L_{jt} = \left(\frac{1}{\sigma}P_t - \frac{W_t}{Z_t}\right)Y_{jt} \tag{72}$$

We have already computed the value of P_t (equation 67):

$$P_t = \frac{(1 + \alpha_a)\Omega_t}{Z_a} \tag{73}$$

From equation (11), since the labor market clears in this case,

$$W_t = (1 + \alpha_t)\Omega_t \tag{74}$$

So profits can be rewritten as

$$\Lambda_{jt} = \left[\frac{1}{\sigma} - \frac{(1+\alpha_t)Z_a}{(1+\alpha_a)Z_t}\right]P_t Y_{jt} = \left[\frac{1}{\sigma} - \frac{\varphi_t}{\varphi_a}\right]P_t Y_{jt} \tag{75}$$

We see that profits will be positive if shocks are sufficiently small in the precise sense that whatever the shocks,

$$\frac{\varphi_t}{\varphi_a} = \frac{(1+\alpha_t)Z_a}{(1+\alpha_a)Z_t} < \frac{1}{\sigma} \tag{76}$$

10

Inflation and Optimal Interest Rate Rules

10.1 Introduction

In the preceding chapter we studied optimal interest rate rules within the framework of a dynamic stochastic general equilibrium (DSGE) model. In accordance with DSGE tradition, these optimal rules were expressed as functions of the shocks hitting the economy.

However, in recent years, following Taylor's (1993) influential article, many authors have studied interest rate rules where central bank policy is a function of endogenous variables such as inflation. A particularly scrutinized issue has been the response of interest rates to inflation,[1] and notably the Taylor principle, according to which the nominal interest rate should respond more than one for one to inflation.[2]

---

1. The original Taylor (1993) contribution actually introduced both inflation and output as arguments of the interest rate rule, but in subsequent writings the role of output has been overshadowed by that of inflation.

2. The reasoning (e.g., see Taylor 1998) is that if the nominal interest rate responds more than one for one to inflation, the real interest rate will respond positively to inflation, which is supposed to have a beneficial stabilizing influence on the economy. Other aspects of the Taylor principle, connected with the issue of price determinacy, were studied in chapters 4 to 6 above.

In this chapter we will study the issue of optimal interest rate rules when they are expressed as functions of inflation (Taylor rules). Our basic framework for this investigation is a dynamic monetary economy subject to stochastic shocks, such as productivity shocks. We will develop a simple model for which we will be able to compute explicit solutions for the optimal Taylor rules.

For the sake of comparison with the previous chapters we will first, in DSGE style, derive interest rate rules that are functions of shocks only. But, because our main interest in this chapter is in rules expressed as a function of inflation, we will then derive a number of optimal interest rate rules where shocks are replaced by various measures of inflation.

Further, because in this model the "fundamentals" are the shocks, inflation will often appear in such interest rate rules as a "surrogate" for the underlying shocks when these are omitted from the policy function. In that respect the argument of the function can be either expected inflation or current inflation (it could even be some past inflation), and we will examine how well they perform as surrogates.

So we will investigate, for various types of rigidities, a number of interest rate rules where current or expected inflation act as surrogates for the underlying shocks. We will see that the optimal degree of response to inflation depends on numerous factors, like which measure of inflation (current or expected) is used, the nature and degree of price rigidities, and the autocorrelation of shocks. But we will find that the corresponding elasticity can be smaller or greater than one, depending on the values of the relevant parameters, and thus not systematically greater than one.

10.2   The Model

10.2.1   The Agents

We will use the same monetary overlapping generations model with production as in the three previous chapters. Let us summarize it briefly. The economy includes representative firms, households, and the government.

Households of generation t have the following two-period utility:

$$U_t = \alpha \log C_{1t} + \log C_{2t+1} - (1 + \alpha)L_t \tag{1}$$

These households are submitted in each period of their life to a cash-in-advance constraint:

$$M_{1t} \geq P_t C_{1t}, \quad M_{2t+1} \geq P_{t+1} C_{2t+1} \tag{2}$$

The representative firm in period t produces output Y_t with labor L_t via the production function

$$Y_t = Z_t L_t \tag{3}$$

where Z_t is a technological shock common to all firms. Profits, if any, are redistributed to young households, as well as central bank profits.

10.2.2   Government Policy and the Optimality Criterion

As in the preceding chapter fiscal transfers are set equal to zero, in order to obtain an activist monetary policy. So the government has essentially one policy instrument, the nominal interest rate i_t.

In order to evaluate the optimality properties of potential interest rate policies, we will use the same criterion as in previous chapters:

$$V_t = E_t \sum_{s=t-1}^{\infty} \beta^{s-t} U_s \tag{4}$$

As we saw, (4) can be rewritten as

$$V_t = E_t \sum_{s=t}^{\infty} \beta^{s-t} \Delta_s \tag{5}$$

with

$$\Delta_t = \alpha \log C_{1t} + \frac{1}{\beta} \log C_{2t} - (1+\alpha) L_t \tag{6}$$

10.3   Market Equilibrium

Let us recall a number of equilibrium relations from the previous chapter. The following relations are valid in all cases:

$$P_t C_{1t} = \frac{\alpha \Omega_t}{1 + i_t} \tag{7}$$

$$P_t C_{2t} = \Omega_t \tag{8}$$

$$C_{1t} + C_{2t} = Y_t = Z_t L_t \tag{9}$$

If the labor market clears,

$$W_t = (1 + \alpha)\Omega_t \tag{10}$$

If the goods market clears, the price is equal to marginal cost:

$$P_t = \frac{W_t}{Z_t} \tag{11}$$

Combining (10) and (11), we find the Walrasian price:

$$P_t^* = (1 + \alpha)\frac{\Omega_t}{Z_t} \tag{12}$$

Since central bank profits and firm profits are redistributed to the households, Ω_t remains constant over time:

$$\Omega_t = \Omega_0 \tag{13}$$

So we combine (12) and (13) to obtain

$$P_t^* = (1 + \alpha)\frac{\Omega_0}{Z_t} \tag{14}$$

We saw in the previous chapter (proposition 9.2) that under Walrasian market clearing the optimal interest rate policy is the "Friedman rule," which consists in keeping the interest rate equal to zero at all times. We next introduce nominal rigidities under the form of preset prices.

10.4   Preset Prices

We now move to the study of economies with nominal rigidities. In order to make the exposition shorter, we will study only price rigidities. We assume preset prices and make the traditional assumption that the preset price is equal to the expected value of the Walrasian price (in logarithms):[3]

$$p_t = E_{t-1}p_t^*$$ (15)

where $p_t = \log P_t$, $p_t^* = \log P_t^*$, and P_t^*, the Walrasian price, is given by equation (14). We note that since the Walrasian price P_t^* does not depend on the interest rate, the preset price P_t will not depend on it either.

10.4.1 Equilibrium Conditions

Since the price is preset, equations (7) and (8) are valid:

$$C_{1t} = \frac{\alpha \Omega_0}{(1 + i_t)P_t}$$ (16)

$$C_{2t} = \frac{\Omega_0}{P_t}$$ (17)

10.4.2 The Optimal Interest Rule

We will now derive the optimal interest rate rule as a function of the technological shocks.

Proposition 10.1 *Under preset prices the optimal interest rate rule is*

$$1 + i_t = \max\left[1, \frac{(1 + \alpha)\Omega_0}{P_t Z_t}\right]$$ (18)

Proof We have to maximize, for all values of the shocks, the quantity

$$\Delta_t = \alpha \log C_{1t} + \frac{1}{\beta} \log C_{2t} - (1 + \alpha)L_t$$ (19)

or, since $C_{1t} + C_{2t} = Z_t L_t$,

3. A more elaborate scheme is studied in section 10.7 below.

$$\Delta_t = \alpha \log C_{1t} + \frac{1}{\beta} \log C_{2t} - (1 + \alpha) \frac{C_{1t} + C_{2t}}{Z_t} \qquad (20)$$

Now, since P_t does not depend on i_t, by (17) C_{2t} does not either. We are left to maximize in i_t for all values of the shocks:

$$\alpha \log C_{1t} - (1 + \alpha) \frac{C_{1t}}{Z_t} \qquad (21)$$

where C_{1t} is given by formula (16). Let us take C_{1t} as an intermediate maximization variable. Maximizing (21), we find that the optimal value for C_{1t} is

$$C_{1t} = \frac{\alpha}{1 + \alpha} Z_t \qquad (22)$$

Equating the two values (16) and (22), and taking into account the fact that i_t must be positive, we find (18). ∎

10.4.3   A Loglinear Version

In what follows we study optimal interest rate rules in loglinearized versions. Ignoring the positivity constraint, we can restate the interest rate rule as follows:

Proposition 10.2   *The loglinearized version of the optimal interest rate rule* (18) *is*

$$i_t = -(z_t - E_{t-1} z_t) \qquad (23)$$

Proof   Loglinearizing (18), and ignoring the positivity condition on i_t, we find

$$i_t = \log[(1 + \alpha)\Omega_0] - p_t - z_t \qquad (24)$$

On the other hand, we saw above (equations 14 and 15) that

$$p_t = E_{t-1} p_t^* = \log[(1 + \alpha)\Omega_0] - E_{t-1} z_t \qquad (25)$$

Combining (24) and (25), we find (23). ∎

Note that in this simple case the optimal interest rate is a function of the innovation of the shock z_t only. In section 10.7 below we will study a more complex pricing scheme where the optimal interest rate depends on all past values of the innovations in z_t.

10.5 Inflation as a Surrogate for Shocks

In propositions 10.1 and 10.2 we considered interest rate rules with technology shocks as arguments. We now move to interest rate rules that are functions of inflation (current or expected) only, and we will see that interest rates will react to inflation notably because inflation acts as a surrogate to shocks.

10.5.1 Equilibrium

Let us recall the values of the preset price equilibrium quantities

$$C_{1t} = \frac{\alpha \Omega_0}{(1 + i_t) P_t} \tag{26}$$

$$C_{2t} = \frac{\Omega_0}{P_t} \tag{27}$$

$$L_t = \frac{\alpha \Omega_0}{(1 + i_t) P_t Z_t} + \frac{\Omega_0}{P_t Z_t} \tag{28}$$

10.5.2 Utility Evaluation

The period t utility is

$$\Delta_t = \alpha \log C_{1t} + \frac{1}{\beta} \log C_{2t} - (1 + \alpha) L_t \tag{29}$$

Inserting (26), (27), and (28) into (29), we obtain the following value for Δ_t:

$$\Delta_t = \alpha \log \left[\frac{\alpha \Omega_0}{(1 + i_t) P_t} \right] + \frac{1}{\beta} \log \left(\frac{\Omega_0}{P_t} \right) - (1 + \alpha) \frac{\Omega_0}{P_t Z_t} \left(\frac{\alpha}{1 + i_t} + 1 \right) \tag{30}$$

or, if we keep only the terms containing the interest rate,

$$\Delta_t = -\log(1 + i_t) - \frac{1 + \alpha}{1 + i_t} \frac{\Omega_0}{P_t Z_t} \tag{31}$$

We can find the optimal interest rate rule by maximizing the expected value of Δ_t (equation 31) with respect to the parameters of the rule. Let us assume the following process for the technology shocks $z_t = \log Z_t$:

$$z_t = \frac{u_t}{1 - \rho \mathcal{L}} \tag{32}$$

where u_t is normal and i.i.d. As indicated above, we will consider two different rules, where the interest rate reacts to current inflation or to expected inflation.

10.5.3 Current Inflation

Let us first consider a rule where the interest rate is a function of current inflation:

$$1 + i_t = A \exp(\phi \pi_t) = A \exp[\phi(p_t - p_{t-1})] \tag{33}$$

Proposition 10.3 *Under preset prices and the technology process* (32), *the optimal interest rate rule is characterized by*

$$\phi = 0 \tag{34}$$

$$A = \exp\left(\frac{\mathcal{V}}{2}\right) \tag{35}$$

$$\mathcal{V} = 1 \tag{36}$$

Proof See the appendix at the end of this chapter. ∎

We see that for the current inflation case the Taylor principle does not hold, since $\phi = 0$. We can now give a simple intuition as to why the coefficient of reaction to inflation ϕ is equal to zero. Let us denote as i_t^* the "optimal" interest rate derived in proposition 10.2. We have, combining

(23) and (32),

$$i_t^* = -u_t \tag{37}$$

On the other hand, we can compute, using formula (25), the expression of current inflation as a function of shocks:

$$\pi_t = p_t - p_{t-1} = -E_{t-1}z_t + E_{t-2}z_{t-1} = -\frac{\rho(1 - \mathcal{L})u_{t-1}}{1 - \rho\mathcal{L}} \tag{38}$$

We see that inflation is function of *past* innovations, whereas the optimal interest rate i_t^* is function of the *current* innovation u_t only. Thus π_t and u_t are statistically independent, so current inflation π_t cannot play the role of a surrogate for u_t; hence the coefficient $\phi = 0$. A nonzero ϕ would only create unwanted "noise," in the statistical sense of the term.

10.5.4 Expected Inflation

Proceeding to the case where the interest rate is a function of expected inflation, we have

$$1 + i_t = A \exp(\phi E_t \pi_{t+1}) = A \exp[\phi E_t(p_{t+1} - p_t)] \tag{39}$$

Proposition 10.4 *Under preset prices and the technology process (32), the optimal interest rate rule is characterized by*

$$\phi = \frac{1 + \rho}{2\rho} \tag{40}$$

$$A = \exp\left(\frac{\nu}{2}\right) \tag{41}$$

$$\nu = \frac{1 - \rho}{2} \tag{42}$$

Proof See the appendix at the end of the chapter. ∎

Notice this time that ϕ is always greater than 1, so the Taylor principle is always verified. To give an intuition about the value of the coefficient ϕ, we can compute the value of expected inflation as a function of shocks:

$$E_t \pi_{t+1} = \pi_{t+1} = p_{t+1} - p_t = -E_t z_{t+1} + E_{t-1} z_t$$

$$= -\frac{\rho(1 - \mathcal{L})u_t}{1 - \rho\mathcal{L}} = -\rho u_t + \frac{\rho(1 - \rho)\mathcal{L}u_t}{1 - \rho\mathcal{L}} \tag{43}$$

Let us separate two cases. First, in the case where $\rho = 1$, expected inflation and the innovation u_t are statistically equivalent, and we have

$$i_t^* = -u_t = E_t \pi_{t+1} \tag{44}$$

so that quite naturally $\phi = 1$.

Now, if $\rho < 1$, $E_t \pi_{t+1}$ contains two terms. The first one, $-\rho u_t$, is collinear to u_t. If there was only this term, the coefficient ϕ would be equal to $1/\rho$. But because of the second term, $\rho(1 - \rho)\mathcal{L}u_t/(1 - \rho\mathcal{L})$, an increase in ϕ creates some inefficient "noise." So in the end the actual coefficient ϕ (equation 40) is between 0 and $1/\rho$.

10.6   Variable Contract Length

We would like now to study the effect of the degree of price rigidity on the coefficient ϕ of response to inflation. The preset price scheme we have been using so far has a fixed duration of one period, and is clearly inadequate for such a study. We will therefore use in this section a different type of contract, inspired by Calvo (1983),[4] and such that the average duration of contracts can take any value between zero and infinity. We will then see that this average duration matters for the determination of the optimal ϕ.

10.6.1   The Price Contracts

In each period s price setters make price commitments for the current period and all periods in the future as well. Following the assumption made

---

4. This variant of the famous Calvo (1983) contract was developed with explicit microeconomic foundations in Bénassy (2002b, 2003a, b). See also Devereux and Yetman (2003) and Mankiw and Reis (2002).

for preset prices, we assume that the price committed in period s for period $t \geq s$, which we denote as p_{st}, is equal to the expectation of the corresponding Walrasian price:[5]

$$p_{st} = E_s(p_t^*) \tag{45}$$

The fundamental feature of these contrats, due to Calvo (1983), is that in each period every price contract has a probability η of being maintained, and a probability $1 - \eta$ of being canceled, in which case it is renegotiated on the basis of the latest information. As a result in each period t the proportion of contracts that have been decided in period $t - j$ is equal to

$$(1 - \eta)\eta^j \tag{46}$$

At time t there coexist many different prices that were decided in past periods $t - j$, $j = 0, 1, \ldots, \infty$. In view of (45), the prices decided in $t - j$ are equal to $E_{t-j}(p_t^*)$, and they are in proportion $(1 - \eta)\eta^j$. As a result p_t (the actual price in period t) is given, up to an unimportant constant, by a weighted average of these previously committed prices, using the weights (46):

$$p_t = (1 - \eta) \sum_{j=0}^{\infty} \eta^j E_{t-j} p_t^* \tag{47}$$

We can also compute, using the same weights, the average duration of these price contracts:

$$\sum_{j=0}^{\infty} (1 - \eta)\eta^j j = \frac{\eta}{1 - \eta} \tag{48}$$

We see that this is quite a flexible formulation, since with an average duration of $\eta/(1 - \eta)$, we can go from full flexibility ($\eta = 0$) to full rigidity ($\eta = 1$).

---

5. In a model with microfoundations the optimally set price differs from (45) by a constant term that depends notably on the market power of the price setter and the amount of uncertainty (Bénassy 2002b, 2003a).

10.6.2   The Optimal Rule: Current Inflation

Recall that the Walrasian price p_t^* is, up to a constant,

$$p_t^* = -z_t \tag{49}$$

Combining (47) and (49), we find that p_t is equal to

$$p_t = -(1 - \eta) \sum_{j=0}^{\infty} \eta^j E_{t-j} z_t \tag{50}$$

We can now characterize the optimal interest rate rule in the case where the interest rate is a function of current inflation.

Proposition 10.5   *Assume that the interest rate rule is function of current inflation:*

$$1 + i_t = A \, \exp(\phi \pi_t) = A \, \exp[\phi(p_t - p_{t-1})] \tag{51}$$

Then the optimal rule is characterized by

$$\phi = \frac{\eta(1 + \rho)}{2(1 - \eta)} \tag{52}$$

Proof   See the appendix at the end of the chapter.   ∎

We see this time that we have a more balanced view than in propositions 10.3 and 10.4, since, depending on the values of η and ρ, the coefficient ϕ may be greater or smaller than 1. So the Taylor principle holds sometimes but not as a general rule.

10.6.3   An Interpretation

As before, we will now compare both the optimal response of interest rates to shocks, and the value of inflation as a function of shocks. The optimal response of interest rates is, up to a constant (see equation 24),

$$i_t^* = -z_t - p_t \tag{53}$$

The shocks are

$$z_t = \frac{u_t}{1 - \rho\mathcal{L}}$$ (54)

Combining (50) and (54), we find the value of the price:

$$p_t = -\frac{(1 - \eta)u_t}{(1 - \rho\mathcal{L})(1 - \eta\rho\mathcal{L})}$$ (55)

From (53) we find the best response of the interest rate:

$$i_t^* = -\frac{u_t}{1 - \rho\mathcal{L}} + \frac{(1 - \eta)u_t}{(1 - \rho\mathcal{L})(1 - \eta\rho\mathcal{L})} = -\frac{\eta u_t}{1 - \eta\rho\mathcal{L}}$$ (56)

From (56) we see that this time the interest rate should respond to a weighted average of past innovations in the technology. Let us now compute the value of inflation:

$$\pi_t = (1 - \mathcal{L})p_t = -\frac{(1 - \eta)(1 - \mathcal{L})u_t}{(1 - \rho\mathcal{L})(1 - \eta\rho\mathcal{L})}$$ (57)

We see that if $\rho = 1$, π_t and i_t^* are collinear: $i_t^* = \eta\pi_t/(1 - \eta)$. Therefore

$$\phi = \frac{\eta}{1 - \eta}$$ (58)

This is what formula (52) tells us for $\rho = 1$.

For the case where $\rho < 1$ we could again decompose π_t as the sum of a term proportional to i_t^* and a term orthogonal to it (noise). The computation is easy, but clumsy, and it is therefore omitted here.

10.6.4 The Optimal Rule: Expected Inflation

We will now characterize the optimal interest rate rule in the case where the interest rate is a function of expected inflation. As it turns out, the formula with ρ different from zero is extremely clumsy, so we will restrict ourselves to the case where shocks are uncorrelated:

Proposition 10.6 *Assume that the interest rate rule is function of expected inflation*

$$1 + i_t = A \exp(\phi E_t \pi_{t+1}) = A \exp[\phi E_t(p_{t+1} - p_t)] \qquad (59)$$

and that shocks are uncorrelated ($\rho = 0$). Then the optimal rule is characterized by

$$\phi = \frac{\eta}{1 - \eta} \qquad (60)$$

Proof   See the appendix at the end of the chapter.   ■

We see that depending on the value of η the coefficient ϕ can be smaller or greater than 1. Thus the Taylor principle does not apply as a general rule.

10.7   Conclusions

We constructed in this chapter a dynamic stochastic model for which it is possible to compute simple explicit solutions for optimal interest rate rules. We paid particular attention to the optimal reaction of nominal interest rates to inflation, and notably whether the elasticity of this reaction function should be greater than one (the Taylor principle).

We characterized this elasticity as a function of various underlying factors, like the autocorrelation of shocks, the degree of rigidity of prices, or the measure of inflation (current or expected). We found that the optimal elasticity could be smaller than one as well as greater, so that the Taylor principle holds sometimes but not in general.

10.8   References

This chapter is adapted from Bénassy (2006a).

Contributions deriving optimal interest rate rules from explicit maximization are found, for example, in Rotemberg and Woodford (1997, 1999), Svensson (1997, 1999), Clarida, Gali and Gertler (1999), King and Wolman (1999), Erceg, Henderson, and Levin (2000), Henderson and Kim (2001), and Woodford (2003).

Appendix: Proofs for Chapter 10

Proof of Proposition 10.3

Finding the optimal rule consists in finding the optimal values for the two parameters ϕ and A. Combining (31) and (33), we will maximize with respect to these two parameters the following quantity:

$$E(\Delta_t) = -\log A - E[\phi(p_t - p_{t-1})]$$

$$-\frac{(1+\alpha)\Omega_0}{A} E \exp[-z_t - p_t - \phi(p_t - p_{t-1})] \qquad (61)$$

Combined with (25), this becomes

$$E(\Delta_t) = -\log A - E[\phi(E_{t-1}z_t - E_{t-2}z_{t-1})]$$

$$-\frac{1}{A} \exp[-z_t + E_{t-1}z_t + \phi(E_{t-1}z_t - E_{t-2}z_{t-1})] \qquad (62)$$

Because z_t is normal with zero mean, this simplifies to

$$E(\Delta_t) = -\log A - \frac{1}{A} \exp\left(\frac{\mathcal{V}}{2}\right) \qquad (63)$$

where $\mathcal{V}$ is the variance of the last term into brackets in expression (62). Now we have

$$E_{t-1}z_t = \frac{\rho u_{t-1}}{1 - \rho \mathcal{L}}, \quad E_{t-2}z_{t-1} = \frac{\rho u_{t-2}}{1 - \rho \mathcal{L}} \qquad (64)$$

The term in brackets in (64) is equal to

$$-\frac{u_t}{1 - \rho \mathcal{L}} + \frac{\rho u_{t-1}}{1 - \rho \mathcal{L}} + \frac{\phi \rho u_{t-1}}{1 - \rho \mathcal{L}} - \frac{\phi \rho u_{t-2}}{1 - \rho \mathcal{L}}$$

$$= -u_t + \phi \rho u_{t-1} - \frac{\phi \rho (1 - \rho)}{1 - \rho \mathcal{L}} u_{t-2} \qquad (65)$$

and its variance $\mathcal{V}$ is therefore equal to

$$\mathcal{V} = 1 + \phi^2 \rho^2 + \frac{\phi^2 \rho^2 (1 - \rho)^2}{1 - \rho^2} = 1 + \frac{2\phi^2 \rho^2}{1 + \rho} \tag{66}$$

We see that minimum variance is reached for $\phi = 0$ (equation 34). The corresponding variance is $\mathcal{V} = 1$ (equation 36). Furthermore maximizing (63) in A yields

$$A = \exp\left(\frac{\mathcal{V}}{2}\right) \tag{67}$$

which is equation (35).

Proof of Proposition 10.4

Combining (31) and (39), we will maximize with respect to ϕ and A:

$$E(\Delta_t) = -\log A - E[\phi E_t(p_{t+1} - p_t)]$$

$$-\frac{(1 + \alpha)\Omega_0}{A} E \exp[-z_t - p_t - \phi E_t(p_{t+1} - p_t)] \tag{68}$$

Combined with (25), this yields

$$E(\Delta_t) = -\log A - E[\phi(E_t z_{t+1} - E_{t-1} z_t)]$$

$$-\frac{1}{A} \exp[-z_t + E_{t-1} z_t + \phi(E_t z_{t+1} - E_{t-1} z_t)] \tag{69}$$

Since z_t is normal with zero mean, this simplifies as

$$E(\Delta_t) = -\log A - \frac{1}{A} \exp\left(\frac{\mathcal{V}}{2}\right) \tag{70}$$

where $\mathcal{V}$ is now the variance of the last term into brackets in (69). We have

$$E_{t-1} z_t = \frac{\rho u_{t-1}}{1 - \rho \mathcal{L}}, \quad E_t z_{t+1} = \frac{\rho u_t}{1 - \rho \mathcal{L}} \tag{71}$$

The last term in brackets in (69) is equal to

$$-\frac{u_t}{1-\rho\mathcal{L}}+\frac{\rho u_{t-1}}{1-\rho\mathcal{L}}+\frac{\phi\rho u_t}{1-\rho\mathcal{L}}-\frac{\phi\rho u_{t-1}}{1-\rho\mathcal{L}}$$

$$=-\frac{1-\phi\rho-\rho(1-\phi)\mathcal{L}}{1-\rho\mathcal{L}}u_t=-(1-\phi\rho)u_t-\frac{\phi\rho(1-\rho)}{1-\rho\mathcal{L}}u_{t-1} \qquad (72)$$

so its variance V is equal to

$$V=(1-\phi\rho)^2+\frac{\phi^2\rho^2(1-\rho)^2}{1-\rho^2}=(1-\phi\rho)^2+\frac{\phi^2\rho^2(1-\rho)}{1+\rho} \qquad (73)$$

Minimization with respect to ϕ yields

$$\phi=\frac{1+\rho}{2\rho} \qquad (74)$$

which is equation (40). Inserting (74) into (73), we obtain the resulting variance:

$$V=\left(1-\frac{1+\rho}{2\rho}\right)^2+\left(\frac{1+\rho}{2\rho}\right)^2\frac{1-\rho}{1+\rho}=\frac{1-\rho}{2} \qquad (75)$$

which is equation (42). Finally maximizing expected utility (70) with respect to the constant term A yields

$$A=\exp\left(\frac{V}{2}\right) \qquad (76)$$

which is equation (41).

Proof of Proposition 10.5

From (32) and (50) the price is equal to

$$p_t=-(1-\eta)\sum_{j=0}^{\infty}\eta^j E_{t-j}z_t=-(1-\eta)\sum_{j=0}^{\infty}\frac{\eta^j\rho^j u_{t-j}}{1-\rho\mathcal{L}}$$

$$= -\frac{(1-\eta)u_t}{(1-\rho\mathcal{L})(1-\eta\rho\mathcal{L})} \tag{77}$$

We want to minimize

$$E\exp[-z_t - p_t - \phi(p_t - p_{t-1})]$$

$$= E\exp\left[-\frac{u_t}{1-\rho\mathcal{L}} + \frac{(1-\eta)u_t}{(1-\rho\mathcal{L})(1-\eta\rho\mathcal{L})} + \frac{\phi(1-\eta)(1-\mathcal{L})u_t}{(1-\rho\mathcal{L})(1-\eta\rho\mathcal{L})}\right]$$

$$= E\exp\left[\frac{-\eta u_t}{1-\eta\rho\mathcal{L}} + \frac{\phi(1-\eta)(1-\mathcal{L})u_t}{(1-\rho\mathcal{L})(1-\eta\rho\mathcal{L})}\right] \tag{78}$$

Now

$$\frac{(1-\eta)(1-\mathcal{L})}{(1-\rho\mathcal{L})(1-\eta\rho\mathcal{L})} = \frac{1}{\rho}\left[\frac{1-\eta\rho}{1-\eta\rho\mathcal{L}} - \frac{1-\rho}{1-\rho\mathcal{L}}\right] \tag{79}$$

so the expression in (78) is equal to

$$E\exp\left[\frac{-\eta u_t}{1-\eta\rho\mathcal{L}} + \left(\frac{1-\eta\rho}{1-\eta\rho\mathcal{L}} - \frac{1-\rho}{1-\rho\mathcal{L}}\right)\frac{\phi u_t}{\rho}\right]$$

$$= E\exp\left[\frac{\phi(1-\eta\rho)-\eta\rho}{\rho(1-\eta\rho\mathcal{L})}u_t - \frac{\phi(1-\rho)}{\rho(1-\rho\mathcal{L})}u_t\right] \tag{80}$$

We want to minimize the variance of the quantity in brackets. The term of order j in the brackets in (80) is equal to

$$\frac{\phi(1-\eta\rho)-\eta\rho}{\rho}\eta^j\rho^j u_{t-j} - \frac{\phi(1-\rho)}{\rho}\rho^j u_{t-j} \tag{81}$$

The variance of the term of order j is, omitting the ρ in the denominator,

$$[\phi(1-\eta\rho)-\eta\rho]^2\eta^{2j}\rho^{2j} + \phi^2(1-\rho)^2\rho^{2j}$$

$$-2\phi(1-\rho)[\phi(1-\eta\rho)-\eta\rho]\eta^j\rho^{2j} \tag{82}$$

Summing over all values of j from zero to infinity, we find the total variance

$$\frac{[\phi(1-\eta\rho)-\eta\rho]^2}{1-\eta^2\rho^2} + \frac{\phi^2(1-\rho)^2}{1-\rho^2} - \frac{2\phi(1-\rho)[\phi(1-\eta\rho)-\eta\rho]}{1-\eta\rho^2} \quad (83)$$

Differentiating with respect to ϕ yields the first-order condition

$$\frac{\phi(1-\eta\rho)-\eta\rho}{1+\eta\rho} + \frac{\phi(1-\rho)}{1+\rho} - \frac{(1-\rho)[2\phi(1-\eta\rho)-\eta\rho]}{1-\eta\rho^2} = 0 \quad (84)$$

Let us factor the coefficient ϕ:

$$\phi\left[\frac{1-\eta\rho}{1+\eta\rho} + \frac{1-\rho}{1+\rho} - \frac{2(1-\rho)(1-\eta\rho)}{1-\eta\rho^2}\right] = \eta\rho\left[\frac{1}{1+\eta\rho} - \frac{1-\rho}{1-\eta\rho^2}\right] \quad (85)$$

Now

$$\frac{1}{1+\eta\rho} - \frac{1-\rho}{1-\eta\rho^2} = \frac{\rho(1-\eta)}{(1+\eta\rho)(1-\eta\rho^2)} \quad (86)$$

$$\frac{1-\eta\rho}{1+\eta\rho} - \frac{(1-\rho)(1-\eta\rho)}{1-\eta\rho^2} = \frac{\rho(1-\eta\rho)(1-\eta)}{(1+\eta\rho)(1-\eta\rho^2)} \quad (87)$$

$$\frac{1-\rho}{1+\rho} - \frac{(1-\rho)(1-\eta\rho)}{1-\eta\rho^2} = \frac{\rho(1-\rho)(\eta-1)}{(1+\rho)(1-\eta\rho^2)} \quad (88)$$

Combining equations (85) to (88), we obtain

$$\phi\left[\frac{1-\eta\rho}{1+\eta\rho} - \frac{1-\rho}{1+\rho}\right] = \frac{\eta\rho}{1+\eta\rho} \quad (89)$$

which simplifies as

$$\phi = \frac{\eta(1+\rho)}{2(1-\eta)} \quad (90)$$

This is formula (52).

Proof of Proposition 10.6

From (32) and (50), with $\rho = 0$, the price is equal to

$$p_t = -(1 - \eta)u_t \qquad (91)$$

We want to minimize

$$E \exp[-z_t - p_t - \phi(E_t p_{t+1} - p_t)] \qquad (92)$$

Now

$$-z_t - p_t = -\eta u_t \qquad (93)$$

$$E_t p_{t+1} = 0 \qquad (94)$$

So the expression in brackets in (92) is equal to

$$-z_t - p_t - \phi(E_t p_{t+1} - p_t) = (\phi\eta - \eta - \phi)u_t \qquad (95)$$

We want to minimize with respect to ϕ the variance of this quantity, meaning $(\phi\eta - \eta - \phi)^2 \sigma_u^2$. This minimum will occur for

$$\phi = \frac{\eta}{1 - \eta} \qquad (96)$$

which is equation (60).

Bibliography

Abel, Andrew B. (1987). Optimal monetary growth. *Journal of Monetary Economics* 19: 437–50.

Allais, Maurice (1947). *Economie et Intérêt*. Paris: Imprimerie Nationale.

Andersen, Torben M. (1986a). Differential information and the role for an active stabilization policy. *Economica* 53: 321–38.

Andersen, Torben M. (1986b). Pre-set prices, differential information and monetary policy. *Oxford Economic Papers* 38: 456–80.

Barro, Robert J. (1974). Are government bonds net wealth? *Journal of Political Economy* 82: 1095–1117.

Bénassy, Jean-Pascal (1995). Money and wage contracts in an optimizing model of the business cycle. *Journal of Monetary Economics* 35: 303–15.

Bénassy, Jean-Pascal (2000). Price level determinacy under a pure interest rate peg. *Review of Economic Dynamics* 3: 194–211.

Bénassy, Jean-Pascal (2001). On the optimality of activist policies with a less informed government. *Journal of Monetary Economics* 47: 45–59.

Bénassy, Jean-Pascal (2002a). Optimal monetary and fiscal policies under wage and price rigidities. *Macroeconomic Dynamics* 6: 429–41.

Bénassy, Jean-Pascal (2002b). *The Macroeconomics of Imperfect Competition and Nonclearing Markets: A Dynamic General Equilibrium Approach*. Cambridge: MIT Press.

Bénassy, Jean-Pascal (2002c). Rigidités nominales dans les modèles d'équilibre général intertemporel stochastique. *L'Actualité économique* 78: 423–57.

Bénassy, Jean-Pascal (2003a). Staggered contracts and persistence: Microeconomic foundations and macroeconomic dynamics. *Louvain Economic Review* 69: 125–44.

Bénassy, Jean-Pascal (2003b). Output and inflation dynamics under price and wage staggering: analytical results. *Annales d'Economie et de Statistique* 69: 1–30.

Bénassy, Jean-Pascal (2003c). Fiscal policy and optimal monetary rules in a non-Ricardian economy. *Review of Economic Dynamics* 6: 498–512.

Bénassy, Jean-Pascal (2004). The fiscal theory of the price level puzzle: A non Ricardian view. Paris: Cepremap, forthcoming in *Macroeconomic Dynamics*.

Bénassy, Jean-Pascal (2005). Interest rate rules, price determinacy and the value of money in a non-Ricardian world. *Review of Economic Dynamics* 8: 651–67.

Bénassy, Jean-Pascal (2006a). Interest rate rules, inflation and the Taylor principle: An analytical exploration. *Economic Theory* 27: 143–62.

Bénassy, Jean-Pascal (2006b). Liquidity effects in non-Ricardian Economies. *Scandinavian Journal of Economics* 108: 65–80.

Bénassy, Jean-Pascal, and Michel Guillard (2005). The Taylor principle and global determinacy in a non Ricardian world. PSE and Université d'Evry.

Benhabib, Jess, Stephanie Schmitt-Grohé, and Martin Uribe (2001a). The perils of Taylor rules. *Journal of Economic Theory* 96: 40–69.

Benhabib, Jess, Stephanie Schmitt-Grohé, and Martin Uribe (2001b). Monetary policy and multiple equilibria. *American Economic Review* 91: 167–86.

Benhabib, Jess, Stephanie Schmitt-Grohé, and Martin Uribe (2002). Avoiding liquidity traps. *Journal of Political Economy* 110: 535–63.

Blanchard, Olivier J. (1985). Debts, deficits and finite horizons. *Journal of Political Economy* 93: 223–47.

Blanchard, Olivier J., and Charles M. Kahn (1980). The solution of linear difference models under rational expectations. *Econometrica* 48: 1305–11.

Brock, William A. (1974). Money and growth: The case of long run perfect foresight. *International Economic Review* 15: 750–77.

Brock, William A. (1975). A simple perfect foresight monetary model. *Journal of Monetary Economics* 1: 133–50.

Buiter, Willem H. (1988). Death, birth, productivity growth and debt neutrality. *Economic Journal* 98: 279–93.

Buiter, Willem H. (2002). The fiscal theory of the price level: A critique. *Economic Journal* 112: 459–80.

Calvo, Guillermo (1983). Staggered prices in a utility-maximizing framework. *Journal of Monetary Economics* 12: 383–98.

Chari, V. V., Lawrence J. Christiano, and Patrick Kehoe (1991). Optimal fiscal and monetary policy: Some recent results. *Journal of Money, Credit and Banking* 23: 519–39.

Christiano, Lawrence J., and Martin Eichenbaum (1992). Liquidity effects and the monetary transmission mechanism. *American Economic Review* 82: 346–53.

Christiano, Lawrence J., Martin Eichenbaum, and Charles L. Evans (1997). Sticky price and limited participation models of money: A comparison. *European Economic Review* 41: 1201–49.

Clarida, Richard, Jordi Gali, and Mark Gertler (1999). The science of monetary policy: A new Keynesian perspective. *Journal of Economic Literature* 38: 1661–1707.

Clower, Robert W. (1967). A reconsideration of the microfoundations of monetary theory. *Western Economic Journal* 6: 1–9.

Cushing, Matthew J. (1999). The indeterminacy of prices under interest rate pegging: The non-Ricardian case. *Journal of Monetary Economics* 44: 131–48.

Devereux, Michael B., and James Yetman (2003). Predetermined prices and the persistent effects of money on output. *Journal of Money, Credit and Banking* 35: 729–41.

Diamond, Peter A. (1965). National debt in a neoclassical growth model. *American Economic Review* 55: 1126–50.

Dixit, Avinash K., and Joseph E. Stiglitz (1977). Monopolistic competition and optimum product diversity. *American Economic Review* 67: 297–308.

Dornbusch, Rudiger, and Jacob A. Frenkel (1973). Inflation and growth: Alternative approaches. *Journal of Money, Credit and Banking* 5: 141–56.

Erceg, Christopher J., Dale W. Henderson, and Andrew T. Levin (2000). Optimal monetary policy with staggered wage and price contracts. *Journal of Monetary Economics* 46: 281–313.

Friedman, Milton (1969). The optimum quantity of money. In M. Friedman, ed., *The Optimum Quantity of Money and Other Essays*. London: Macmillan, pp. 1–50.

Fuerst, Thomas S. (1992). Liquidity, loanable funds and real activity. *Journal of Monetary Economics* 29: 3–24.

Gale, David (1973). Pure exchange equilibrium of dynamic economic models. *Journal of Economic Theory* 6: 12–36.

Grandmont, Jean-Michel, and Yves Younès (1973). On the efficiency of a monetary equilibrium. *Review of Economic Studies* 40: 149–65.

Gray, Jo-Anna (1976). Wage indexation: A macroeconomic approach. *Journal of Monetary Economics* 2: 221–35.

Guillard, Michel (2004). Politique monétaire et fiscale dans un monde non-Ricardien: Une théorie fiscale de l'inflation. Université d'Evry.

Helpman, Elhanan (1981). An exploration in the theory of exchange-rate regimes. *Journal of Political Economy* 89: 865–90.

Henderson, Dale W., and Jinill Kim (2001). The choice of a monetary policy reaction function in a simple optimizing model. In A. Leijonhufvud, ed., *Monetary Theory and Policy Experience*. London: Macmillan.

Hicks, John R. (1937). Mr Keynes and the "classics": A suggested interpretation. *Econometrica* 5: 147–59.

Jeanne, Olivier (1994). Nominal rigidities and the liquidity effect. Paris: CERAS.

Keynes, John Maynard (1936). *The General Theory of Employment, Interest and Money*. New York: Harcourt Brace.

King, Robert G. (1982). Monetary policy and the information content of prices. *Journal of Political Economy* 90: 247–79.

King, Robert G. (1983). Interest rates, aggregate information, and monetary policy. *Journal of Monetary Economics* 12: 199–234.

King, Robert G., and Alexander L. Wolman (1999). What should the monetary authority do when prices are sticky. In J. B. Taylor, ed., *Monetary Policy Rules*. Chicago: University of Chicago Press.

Kocherlakota, Narayana, and Christopher Phelan (1999). Explaining the fiscal theory of the price level. *Federal Reserve Bank of Minneapolis Quarterly Review* 23(4): 14–23.

Leeper, Eric M. (1991). Equilibria under "active" and "passive" monetary and fiscal policies. *Journal of Monetary Economics* 27: 129–47.

Lucas, Robert E., Jr. (1972). Expectations and the neutrality of money. *Journal of Economic Theory* 4: 103–24.

Lucas, Robert E., Jr. (1982). Interest rates and currency prices in a two-country world. *Journal of Monetary Economics* 10: 335–59.

Lucas, Robert E., Jr. (1990). Liquidity and interest rates. *Journal of Economic Theory* 50: 237–64.

Lucas, Robert E., Jr., and Nancy L. Stokey (1983). Optimal fiscal and monetary policy in an economy without capital. *Journal of Monetary Economics* 12: 55–93.

Mankiw, N. Gregory, and Ricardo Reis (2002). Sticky information versus sticky prices: A proposal to replace the new-Keynesian Phillips curve. *Quarterly Journal of Economics* 117: 1295–1328.

McCallum, Bennett T. (1981). Price level determinacy with an interest rate policy rule and rational expectations. *Journal of Monetary Economics* 8: 319–29.

McCallum, Bennett T. (1986). Some issues concerning interest rate pegging, price level determinacy and the real bills doctrine. *Journal of Monetary Economics* 17: 135–60.

McCallum, Bennett T. (1999). Issues in the design of monetary policy rules. In J. B. Taylor and M. Woodford, eds., *Handbook of Macroeconomics*. Amsterdam: North Holland.

McCallum, Bennett T. (2001). Indeterminacy, bubbles, and the fiscal theory of price level determination. *Journal of Monetary Economics* 47: 19–30.

Muth, John F. (1961). Rational expectations and the theory of price movements. *Econometrica* 29: 315–35.

Niepelt, Dirk (2004). The fiscal myth of the price level. *Quarterly Journal of Economics* 119: 277–300.

Patinkin, Don (1956). *Money, Interest and Prices*, 2nd ed. New York: Harper and Row.

Phillips, A. W. (1958). The relationship between unemployment and the rate of change of money wages in the United Kingdom, 1861–1957. *Economica* 25: 283–99.

Pigou, Arthur C. (1943). The classical stationary state. *Economic Journal* 53: 343–51.

Ramsey, Frank P. (1928). A mathematical theory of saving. *Economic Journal* 38: 543–59.

Roisland, O. (2003). Capital income taxation, equilibrium determinacy and the Taylor principle. *Economics Letters* 81: 147–53.

Rotemberg, Julio J. (1982a). Monopolistic price adjustment and agregate output. *Review of Economic Studies* 44: 517–31.

Rotemberg, Julio J. (1982b). Sticky prices in the United States. *Journal of Political Economy* 90: 1187–1211.

Rotemberg, Julio J. (1987). The new Keynesian microfoundations. *NBER Macroeconomics Annual* 2: 69–104.

Rotemberg, Julio J., and Michael Woodford (1997). An optimization based econometric framework for the evaluation of monetary policy. *NBER Macroeconomics Annual* 12: 297–346.

Rotemberg, Julio J., and Michael Woodford (1999). Interest rate rules in an estimated sticky price model. In J. B. Taylor, ed., *Monetary Policy Rules*. Chicago: University of Chicago Press.

Samuelson, Paul A. (1958). An exact consumption-loan model of interest with or without the social contrivance of money. *Journal of Political Economy* 66: 467–82.

Samuelson, Paul A. (1967). A turnpike refutation of the golden rule in a welfare-maximizing many-year plan. In K. Shell, ed., *Essays on the Theory of Optimal Economic Growth*. Cambridge: MIT Press.

Samuelson, Paul A. (1968). The two-part golden rule deduced as the asymptotic turnpike of catenary motions. *Western Economic Journal* 6: 85–89.

Sargent, Thomas J., and Neil Wallace (1975). Rational expectations, the optimal monetary instrument and the optimal money supply rule. *Journal of Political Economy* 83: 241–54.

Sidrauski, Miguel (1967). Rational choices and patterns of growth in a monetary economy. *American Economic Review* 57: 534–44.

Sims, Christopher A. (1994). A simple model for the determination of the price level and the interaction of monetary and fiscal policy. *Economic Theory* 4: 381–99.

Svensson, Lars E. O. (1997). Inflation forecast targeting: implementing and monitoring inflation targets. *European Economic Review* 41: 1111–46.

Svensson, Lars E. O. (1999). Inflation targeting as a monetary policy rule. *Journal of Monetary Economics* 43: 607–54.

Taylor, John B. (1993). Discretion versus policy rules in practice. *Carnegie-Rochester Series on Public Policy* 39: 195–214.

Taylor, John B. (1998). Monetary policy and the long boom. *Federal Reserve Bank of Saint-Louis Review* 80(6): 3–11.

Taylor, John B., ed. (1999). *Monetary Policy Rules.* Chicago: University of Chicago Press.

Turnovsky, Stephen J. (1980). The choice of monetary instrument under alternative forms of price expectations. *Manchester School* 48: 39–62.

Wallace, Neil (1980). The overlapping generations model of fiat money. In J. Kareken and N. Wallace, eds., *Models of Monetary Economies.* Minneapolis: Federal Reserve Bank of Minneapolis, pp. 49–82.

Weil, Philippe (1987). Permanent budget deficits and inflation. *Journal of Monetary Economics* 20: 393–410.

Weil, Philippe (1989). Overlapping families of infinitely-lived agents. *Journal of Public Economics* 38: 183–98.

Weil, Philippe (1991). Is money net wealth? *International Economic Review* 32: 37–53.

Weil, Philippe (2002). Reflections on the fiscal theory of the price level. ECARES and ULB.

Weiss, Laurence (1980). The role for active monetary policy in a rational expectations model. *Journal of Political Economy* 88: 221–33.

Woodford, Michael (1994). Monetary policy and price level determinacy in a cash-in-advance economy. *Economic Theory* 4: 345–80.

Woodford, Michael (1995). Price level determinacy without control of a monetary aggregate. *Carnegie-Rochester Conference Series on Public Policy* 43: 1–46.

Woodford, Michael (1999). Price level determination under interest-rate rules. Princeton University.

Woodford, Michael (2003). *Interest and Prices: Foundations of a Theory of Monetary Policy.* Princeton: Princeton University Press.

Yaari, Menahem E. (1965). Uncertain lifetime, life insurance, and the theory of the consumer. *Review of Economic Studies* 32: 137–50.

Index